THE WORKBENCH TREASURY OF Coffee, Tea & Serving Table Projects

for the HOME CRAFTSMAN

by the Staff of WORKBENCH Magazine

Modern Handcraft, Inc.
Kansas City

Copyright 1981 Modern Handcraft, Inc.

All Rights Reserved. No part of this work may be reproduced without written permission from the publisher, except by a reviewer who may quote short passages in a review with appropriate credits.

ATTENTION: SCHOOLS AND BUSINESS FIRMS
Modern Handcraft books are available at quantity discounts for bulk purchases for educational, business or sales promotional use.

All inquiries should be addressed to Modern Handcraft, Inc.
4251 Pennsylvania, Kansas City, Missouri 64111

Printed in the United States of America

Library of Congress Cataloging in Publication Data
Main entry under title:
The Workbench treasury of coffee, tea, and serving table projects for the home craftsman.
1. Tables. I. Workbench.
II. Title: Coffee, tea, and serving table projects for the home craftsman.
TT197.5.T3W67   684.1'3   81-80204
ISBN 0-86675-002-9   AACR2

Contents

Introduction 4
Traditional cobbler's bench coffee table 6
Rustic wagon seat coffee table 8
Rough-hewn, slab-top coffee table 9
Sculptured slab-top coffee table 12
Wine-rack base coffee table 13
Simple display-top coffee table 14
Octagonal display case coffee table 15
Display coffee table with cabinet 16
John-boy coffee table 18
Burn-finished coffee table 19
Rugged cedar and pine coffee table 20
Ceramic tile Spanish style coffee table 21
Colonial style table with modern tile-top 22
Hide-away wine cabinet coffee table 23
Danish modern coffee table 26
Quick-and-easy coffee table 28
Basket weave-top coffee table 29
Sculptured, glass-topped coffee table 30
Wrought iron base coffee table 32
Triangular cherrywood coffee table 33
English butler-tray serving table 36
Basic tea cart 37
Colonial style serving cart 39
Contemporary Danish tea cart 41
Chippendale-Chinese style tea cart 43
Colonial tea table with cabriole legs 46
Elegant Queen Anne table 47

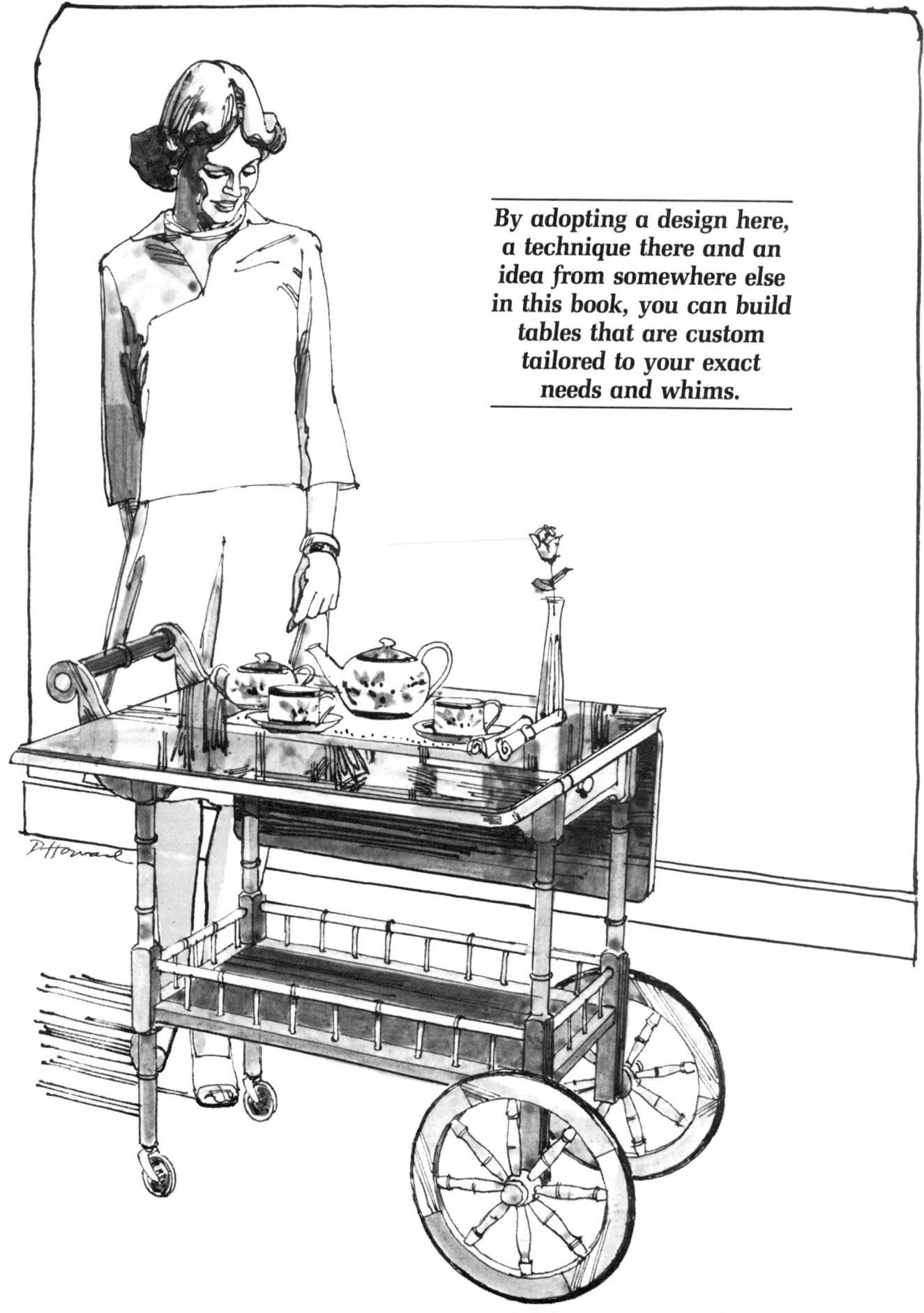

By adopting a design here, a technique there and an idea from somewhere else in this book, you can build tables that are custom tailored to your exact needs and whims.

Introduction

The purpose of this book is to introduce the home craftsman to a wide variety of coffee tables, tea tables and serving tables that can be built at home. Gleaned from over 20 years of WORKBENCH Magazine table plans, these particular tables were chosen to provide the reader with an abundant array of different table styles, construction techniques, and degrees of difficulty to challenge one's woodworking expertise.

All of the tables shown can be made with basic hand tools, as all furniture was crafted for centuries. However, those home craftsmen who have one or more power tools can often do the job faster, easier and in some instances, with more precision. Care was taken to include a fair range of stylings such as extremely simple "orange-crate" designs for the eager beginner, rough hewn "John-boy" designs for the rugged individualist, the delicate artistry of classic antique designs for the accomplished woodworker, and the like.

It isn't possible to present here examples of every conceivable design, period, type, size, shape and style of coffee, tea or serving table, because the list would be endless. Instead, you will find a goodly cross-section to be used as an idea treasury for good reason. Give any ten craftsmen identical sets of table plans and when the tables are finished you will see ten different tables. Why? Because each woodworker has a different degree of skill, uses different tools, perhaps employs his own techniques, adds his own ideas and innovations, and certainly is motivated by his own individual tastes and desires.

For example, such master cabinetmakers as Robert Adams, Duncan Phyfe, Thomas Sheraton and George Hepplewhite, whose individualistic styles have become classic, all were at one time apprentices, then journeymen at woodworking. Their handcrafted pieces now are priceless antiques. Each of these 18th century craftsmen played a major part in a breakaway from the traditional Chippendale styling which they'd been taught. Yet each one of these men pioneered a particular styling that was so artistically unique as to earn each of them a place in furniture history.

By adopting a design here, a technique there and an idea from somewhere else in this book, you can build tables that are custom tailored to your exact needs and whims. That's a luxury you seldom find in rubber-stamp, factory-made furniture.

Another objective of this book is to include home-made examples of tables influenced by the "Art Deco" furniture stylings of the twenties and thirties that made the most of salvaged pieces, unlikely and innovative materials, and found objects. Thus, as you will see, this book encourages you to choose that which best fits your budget, needs, tools and expertise. And you also are encouraged to satisfy your hunger for creativity or desire for artistic expression by daring to be original.

Whenever possible highly technical language has been avoided. Plans, diagrams and photos are provided so every table shown can actually be built. In most cases explanations purposely are kept short, except where more detailed, step-by-step instructions are needed to illustrate particular techniques or the construction of more sophisticated tables. It's realistic to assume that the home craftsman already has a good grasp of common construction details, simple assembly procedures, how to read and interpret plans, what tools to use for a particular result, how to finish furniture, and so forth.

And, it goes without saying that no table is irrevocably committed to the particular type of wood specified in an example, and thus you are encouraged to select that wood which is more convenient or preferable to you. Where shopping lists are given, keep in mind that lumber companies and other wood suppliers often are better equipped than home craftsmen to cut lumber purchases to exact dimension, thus saving you time and effort.

One final note. Fine woods, special hardware, and the like aren't always readily available locally. Thousands of home craftsmen find regular advertisers in WORKBENCH Magazine to be dependable sources of supply.

Traditional cobbler's bench coffee table

Used as a coffee table, the cobbler's bench is one of the more colorful and practical adaptations of early Americana. The bench shown is a faithful reproduction of an existing one and will enhance the beauty of any room with colonial decor.

Start construction by making the top. This should be glued-up from two or more pieces to minimize chances of its warping. Shape the seat depression—which can be done with a disk sander—and sand it smooth. Cut a dado 1/4 in. deep x 1/2 in. wide, 6-3/4 in. from the wide end as indicated, to accept the face board for the small drawer section.

Cut out and attach with glue and screws the curved member under the seat end, and the two drawer guides at the opposite end. Holes for the legs now are drilled with the aid of the jig detailed. It is a block of wood 2 in. square and 6 in. long in which a 1 in. hole is drilled. Set the miter gauge and saw arbor at 10 degrees and saw through the hole. The resulting jig is fitted with two strips that are planed at the angle of the cut end. These strips are used to temporarily tack-nail the jig to the underside of the bench top for accurate drilling of the leg holes. Clamp a block of scrap wood to the bench top to prevent the drill from tearing the wood when it goes through.

Cut the legs to size next, making them 1-3/4 x 1-3/4 x 14 in. Into one end of each leg drill a hole 1 in. in diameter x 3 in. deep. At each end of each leg, make a 10 degree x 10 degree compound cut, shortening them to 12-1/8 in. with this operation.

Next, taper the legs from 1-3/4 in. at one end to 1-1/2 in. at the other end. This can be done with a taper jig on a table or radial-arm saw, or on a jointer. Make the dowels and wedges as shown. Add glue, then drive a dowel and wedge into each leg.

Cut the dowels a length that will permit them to project slightly above the bench top. When the glue has set, sand the dowel ends flush with the top. Cut the side and end members next. Dado the end piece horizontally to receive the horizontal partitions that are 1/4 in. longer than the vertical members. The photographs show dovetail joints between the sides and end of the bench, the drawing shows butt joints. If dovetails are used, lengthen the end member by 1-1/2 in. to allow for them.

Drawers are cut and assembled next. Fit each one to its own opening. The larger drawer is fitted to slide easily on the guides under the top. Glue small blocks on the underside of the top to act as stops for the drawer.

Complete the bench by plugging all screw holes, and adding the tool holder, triangular strips and the small strips that form the nail compartments. "Distress" the bench for an antique look, then sand smooth. Add paste filler, wipe off with a cloth, then let dry overnight. Sand with 6/0 paper, then stain. Apply two or three coats of sanding sealer and the bench is finished.

MATERIALS LIST

Top, (glued-up), pine, 1-3/8" x 17-1/2" x 43"
Side, long, 3/4" x 8" x 29"
Side, short, 3/4" x 8" x 21-1/2"
End, 3/4" x 8" x 16-1/2"
Drawers, partitions, 1/2" x 12" x 48" pine, cut to size
Legs, cut from 2 x 12 x 24"
Drawer guides, cut from 1" x 12" x 24" hardwood
Drawer bottoms, cut from 1/4" plywood 24" x 24"
Cut from curved member under seat, 3/4" x 7" x 16"
Leg attachment, 1" dowel x 24"
Knobs, 3/4" white porcelain (4)
Knobs, 1-1/2" white porcelain (1)
Flathead screws, #10 x 1-1/4" (2 doz.)
Flathead screws, #8 x 1-1/4" (3 doz.)

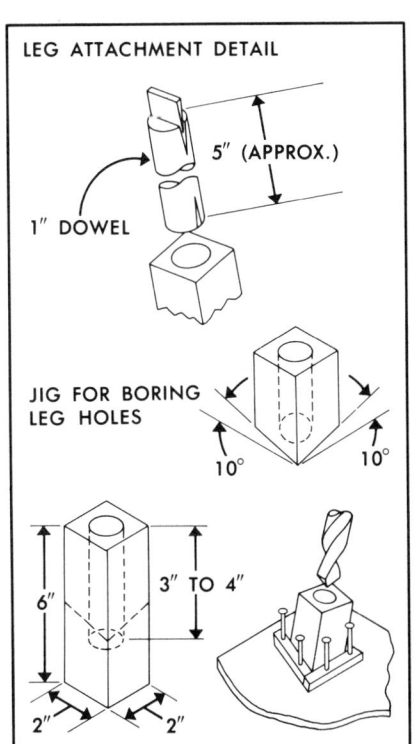

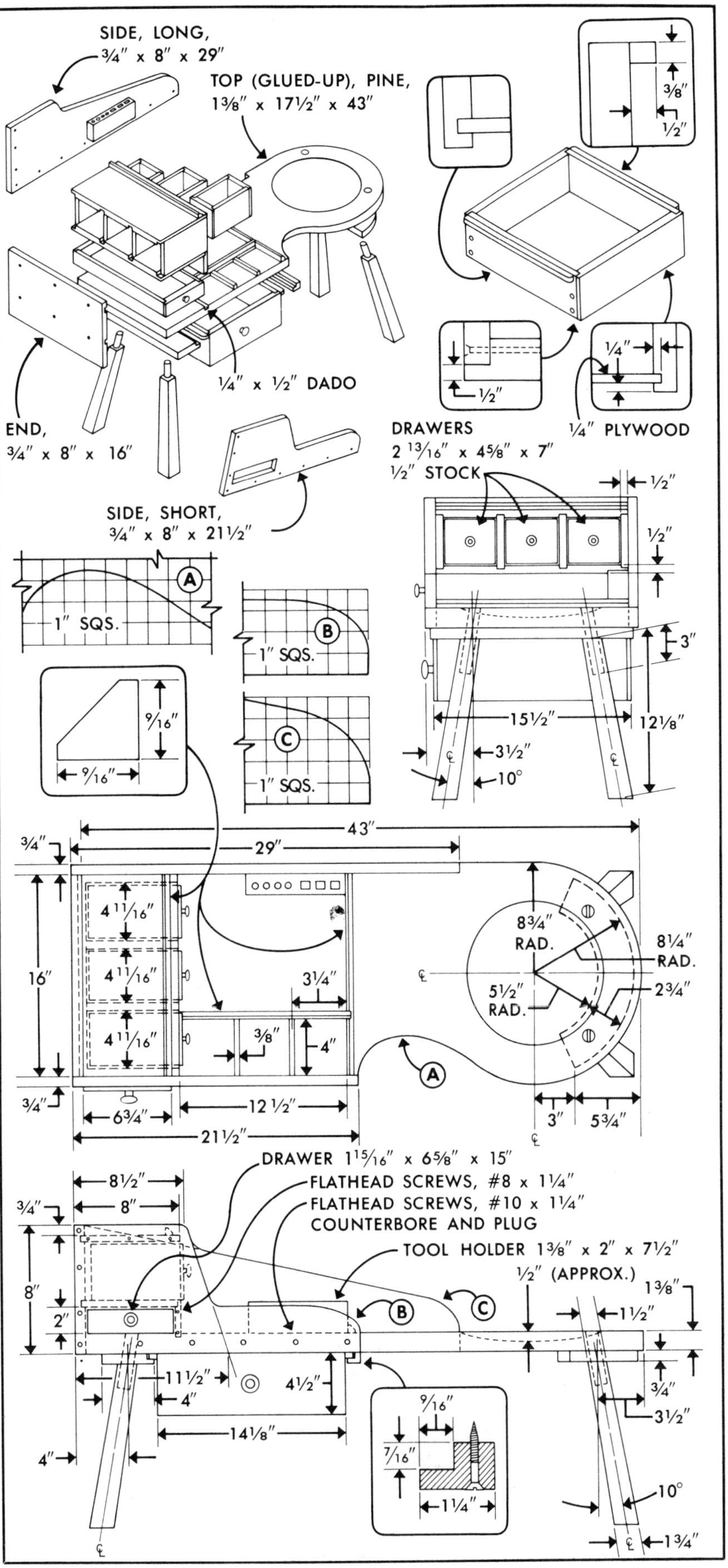

Rustic wagon seat coffee table

One antique in great demand—and short supply—is a wagon or buggy seat. They now are used for everything from informal benches to flower stands to simple decorations for a porch to a coffee table.

This reproduction is authentic in appearance, and can be used for any of the purposes listed. Best of all, it will cost only a few dollars, plus some time in the workshop.

If you can get some weathered lumber, it will add much to the antique look of the project. If not, then distress the lumber by filing all edges to simulate wear, and do a little hammering and battering to create the look of age.

Edge-glue the pieces for the seat, then glue and nail them to the braces that are cut from 2 x 4s. Use square-head flooring nails, or shape the heads of regular nails to look like hand-forged fasteners.

Finished coffee table. Lower shelf holds magazines or books and casters allow table to be moved about with ease. The wagon seat "springs" are stabilized by the vertical rod welded between the leaves.

The sub-assembled wagon seat is sanded smooth prior to applying stain and rubbed-oil finish.

The table feet are being finished here with boiled linseed oil.

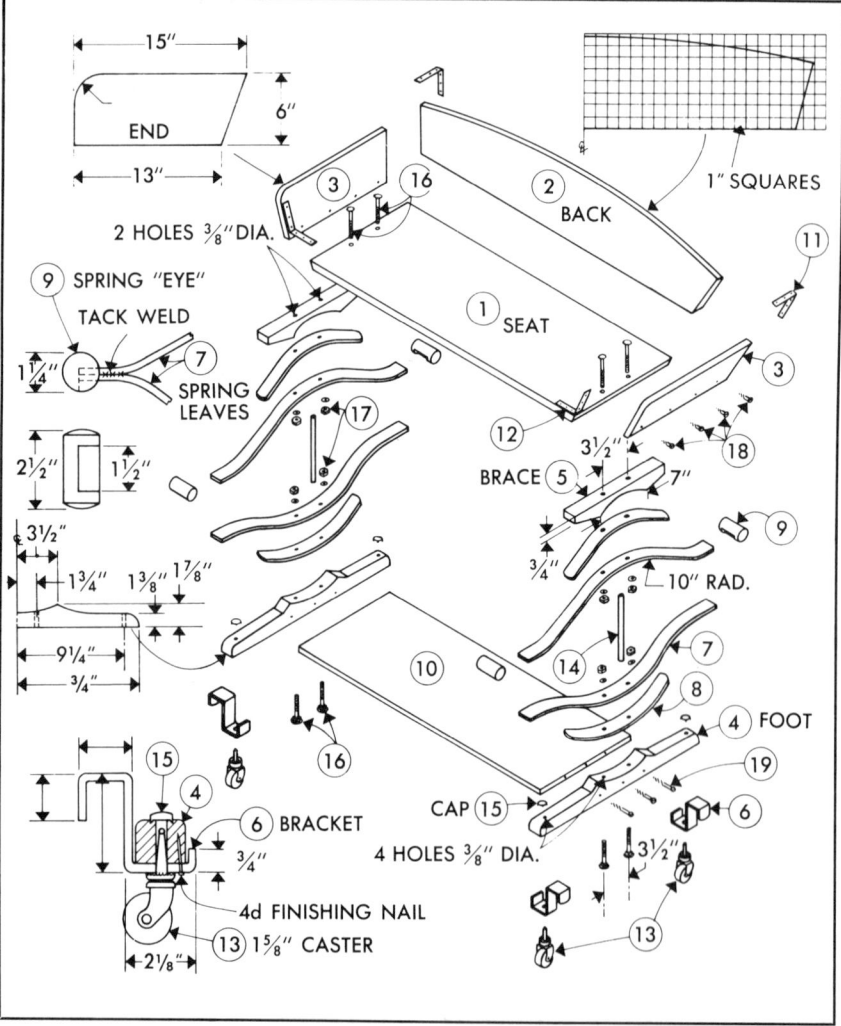

Cut the back and sides from 1 x 8 or 1 x 10 lumber. Glue and nail them to the edges of the seat, allowing the lower edges to project so they can be planed at an angle, flush to the underside of the seat.

Oak, hickory or other tough hardwood is used for the "feet." Attach the feet to the shelf with 2-1/2 in. flathead wood screws.

The leaf "springs" are shaped from flat bar, joined at the ends with a 1-1/4 in. dowel, and reinforced at the center with a 1/2 in. steel rod welded at top and bottom. The springs and all metal parts are painted flat black; one spray can does the job and in a hurry.

Finish the wooden parts to suit your preference or match the room's decor; the original has stain and a rubbed-on linseed oil. You may want an antique with glaze, or even a "Hitchcock" black with gold striping, such as used on new buggies. The casters may not be authentic, but they certainly make it a lot easier to move the table, whether for cleaning or to relocate it in a room.

MATERIALS LIST

Seat, edge-glued 1 x 3s or 1 x 4s x 35-1/4" long
Back, 1 x 8 x 39-3/4" (1)
End, 1 x 8 x 15" (2)
Foot, 1-5/8" x 1-7/8" x 21-1/2" (2)
Brace, 1-3/8" x 1-5/8" x 12" (2)
Bracket, 1/4" x 1-1/2" x 10" steel flat (4)
Spring, 3/16" x 1-1/2" x 30" steel flat (4)
Spring, 1/8" x 1-1/2" x 14" steel flat (4)
Ferrule, 1-1/4" x 2-1/2" dowel (4)
Shelf, 1 x 4 x 32-1/2" (3)
Strap, sheet metal, 5/8" x 7" (2)
Strap, 1/8" x 3/4" x 7" steel flat (2)
Caster, 1-5/8" dia., stem with socket (4)
Rod, 1/2" dia. x 7-1/2" (2)
Cap, chair glide, 3/4" dia. (4)
Carriage bolt, 5/16" x 2-1/2" (8)
Nut, 5/16" hex (8)
Wood screw, #10 x 3/4" FH steel (20)
Wood screw, #10 x 2-1/2" FH steel (6)

LOG ROUND FOR COFFEE TABLE WITH THREE OR FOUR SCREW-ON LEGS

DOUBLE SLAB AS TWO-LEVEL END TABLE

END TABLE WITH OPEN STORAGE FOR BOOKS

Rough-hewn slab-top coffee table

Here's a simple technique for making striking tables, footstools and other decorative items from slabs of rough wood. The focal point of these projects is the finish which is a thick, high-gloss, clear plastic. Simple or complex bases can be made to suit your needs, but the important part of making this type of furniture is achieving a glass-smooth finish.

To make slab furniture you need a dry and reasonably smooth piece of wood 1 to 3 in. thick. The slab need not be sound. As a matter of fact, some of the most attractive tops are made of wood that is in poor condition from rot, splits, missing or broken knots, worm damage, and the like. The tables shown are made of 2 to 2-1/2 in. thick black walnut slabs, but any wood will work fine. The wood you choose may depend on what you prefer in grain pattern or what is available.

A chain saw is great for cutting the slabs. The uneven cut of the saw leaves a nice rustic look to the

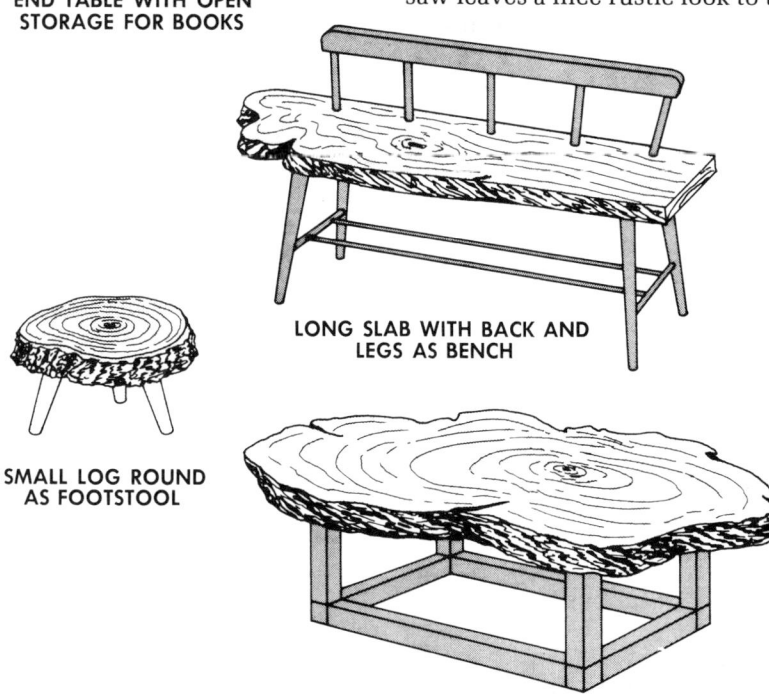

SMALL LOG ROUND AS FOOTSTOOL

LONG SLAB WITH BACK AND LEGS AS BENCH

COMTEMPORARY OPEN-BASE TABLE GLUED UP FROM 2 x 2s

You can make a coffee table similar to this with a slab of wood, and some legs. "Wet look" clear plastic covers top.

Plastic coated log slice and three screw-on furniture legs made this slick new coffee table.

edges when trimming and shaping the wood. An attachment used for cutting lumber with a chain saw would also be helpful in cutting a consistent thickness on long slabs. Generally, round or long and narrow slabs make beautiful coffee tables. Rectangular or oval slabs make nice end and occasional tables.

After the wood is cut, it must be surface planed. If you do not have a surface planer, a cabinet or woodworking shop can do the work for you. Alternately, you can work it down by making multiple passes on a jointer/planer or with a portable sander using successively finer sanding grades. Sand the surface and any sharp edges smooth and remove any loose material that may be in holes and cracks.

Before proceeding with the finish, determine the type of base on which you want to mount the top. Make the base and drill the mounting holes in the slab, but do not attach the top. This will be done when the top is completed.

Now you are ready to finish the slab. The finish is a two-part liquid plastic that is almost water-clear and virtually odorless. The plastic is mixed with equal parts of each solution and sets up rock-hard. Naturally, when using the material, have anything in your work area that you do not want ruined covered with paper or plastic. The first step in finishing is to fill all cracks and voids with the plastic. Due to the refraction of the light, the filled holes take on a dark, solid appearance. When the material has dried, the filled spots are sanded flush with the top, then the surface is tack-ragged clean.

Figure out how slabs can be utilized, which side has nicest grain pattern. Turning over may suggest new ideas.

In determining a use, mark out where the legs or base might locate, figure where trim cuts should be made.

End table is a slice out of a tree crotch, with corners rounded only enough to make it safe.

To prevent the slab from warping, both sides must be coated. Starting with the bottom side, make a tape "dam" around the bottom edge as shown. This will keep the plastic from running down the sides and forming drip globs on the down-side edge.

After mixing thoroughly, the two-part finish is poured on the surface and distributed with a piece of clean, stiff material such as cardboard. It is important that the slab is firmly held as level as possible to prevent the finish from running to one side. Let the plastic dry, then remove the tape and round the edges of the bottom coat with a rasp.

Next, turn the slab over and check for levelness of the top. Tack-rag the surface to remove dust, then mix enough plastic to cover the entire top in one coat. "Trowel" the finish over the surface with a piece of cardboard quickly, smoothing what runs over the edge of the slab. Drips at the bottom edge can be rasped and polished later, when the material is dry. Full curing time is about seventy-two hours at room temperature, so keep the project in an isolated area, free of drafts and especially dust.

Although the plastic is relatively free of bubbles, any that do show up in the finish can be removed by lightly heating the surface with a propane or "flameless" torch soon after the finish is applied.

If you should happen to make a mistake, it is possible to recoat the surface without removing the first finish. Instructions provided with the material normally cover this, along with information on how to fill bad scratches which may happen when the finished piece is in use.

The finished surface has a deep, high gloss "wet" look. It requires no care, but it can be waxed if you so desire. If the slab should become scuffed, it can be buffed with a fine compound such as white automotive polishing compound. If you want to dull the gloss, try rubbing it with automotive rubbing compound.

The top is now ready to be mounted on a base or legs. Perhaps the quickest and easiest is to use screw-on legs, which are readily available, but you may want to spend a little extra time to make something uniquely your own.

If you don't have any slabs of wood or a good saw to cut the slabs, check with your local lumberyards, cabinet shops and sawmills for scraps. They usually have ends and pieces that they are glad to get rid of for a nominal price. And don't overlook trees on your own property. If a tree has to be felled or is downed by a storm, consider having slices cut from the tree and dried.

Unwanted ends can be trimmed off with a chain saw. End itself might be used for another project.

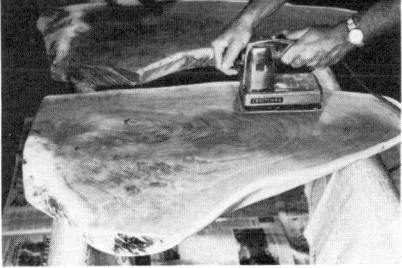

Sand the top surface as smooth as possible and make sure it is dust free before applying plastic.

Use a folded chunk of clean cardboard as a "trowel" to apply plastic. Don't do more than one piece at a time.

Make a tape "dam" around bottom, coat bottom surface with plastic to keep piece from warping later.

Fill every void and crack you can find before applying finish to entire top, to avoid sinkage in final coat.

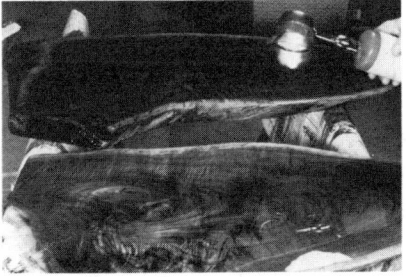

A propane torch or a flameless torch such as the Magna Paint Peeler can be used to remove any bubbles in finish.

Sculptured slab-top coffee table

Although the tabletop shown here was made of Hawaiian monkey pod, a slab of any other wood with an attractive grain pattern such as maple, walnut or redwood would be satisfactory. A burl of either of these would make an exceptionally luxurious looking tabletop.

The overall dimensions are shown in the drawing. Note that this top was made of two slabs of wood, butt-jointed and glued in the middle. Note also that there is not even the hint of bark or rough-hewing, because the whole object of this table is to focus in on the beauty of the wood graining and give it the smooth contouring of polished marble for added dramatic effect.

This tabletop can be made entirely with hand tools. Hand carve the legs from a hardwood such as oak and cut off each end at 10 degrees. A pilot hole for a 1/2 in. lag bolt is drilled parallel to the center line of the stock.

Assemble the leg to the tabletop as shown in the drawing. A recess is bored in the top to receive the bolt heads. The legs first are bolted to the cross members, then the cross members are screwed to the tabletop.

Sand the top and legs thoroughly, wipe off the dust and finish with a tough, durable finish such as bar-top varnish, or use a penetrating-oil sealer.

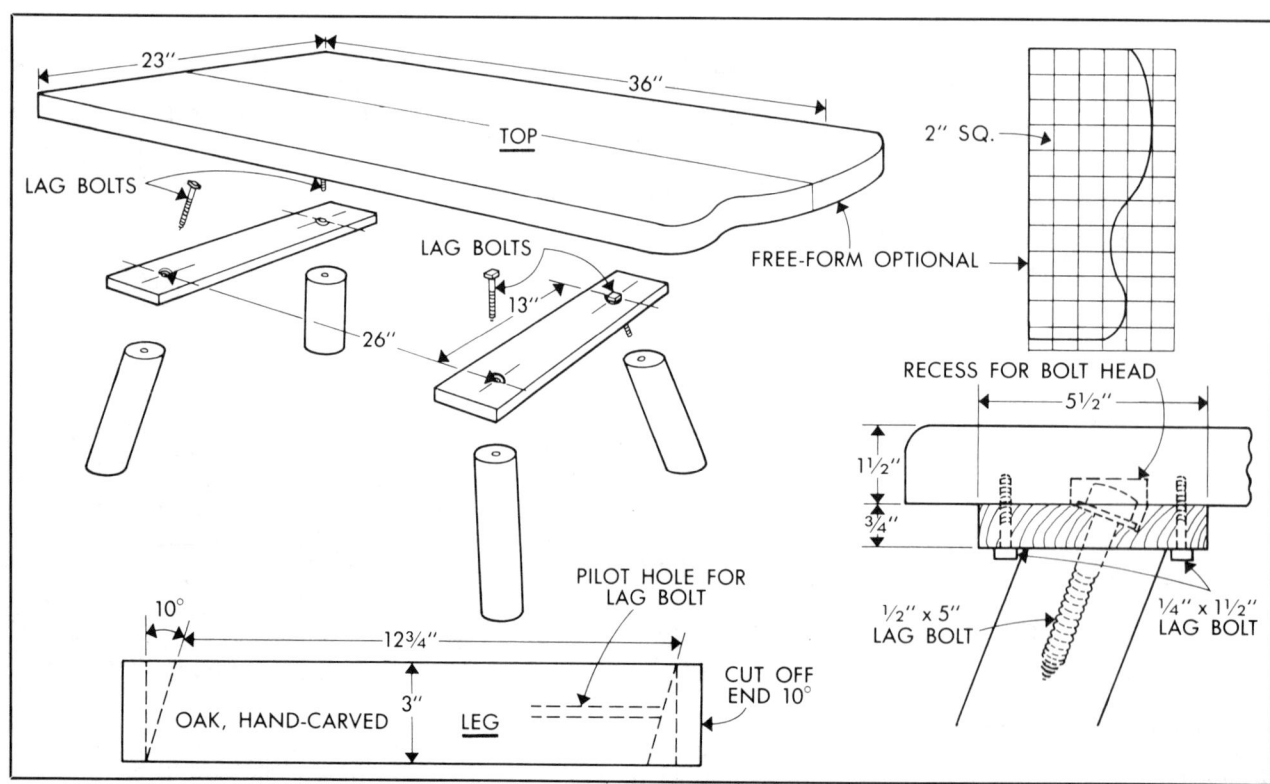

Wine-rack base coffee table

Here's a coffee table for those who want a design that is simple, clean, airy and contemporary.

A length of well-seasoned birch plank that measures 1-3/4 x 12 x 50 in. is ripped on a table saw to make the frames, rails and stiles. Each piece is sanded smooth before being shaped.

To avoid having to lay out each piece, make cardboard patterns of the bottle-neck rail, and the bottle-bottom rail. The stiles are straight lengths measuring 5/8 x 1-1/4 x 18 in., and eight of these are required.

Stack three bottle-neck rails together, mark the pattern on the top one and cut the three to shape in one operation.

The 12 rails you make for the bottle bottoms and necks are rabbeted 5/16 x 1-1/4 in. on each end to fit against the supporting stiles. The rabbets can be made by first cutting across the rails 5/16 in. deep to cut out the 1-1/4 in. width of the rabbet.

When you mark out the rails with the patterns also mark the locations of the several holes. These now are drilled 1/8 in. in diameter, and are countersunk on the sides opposite the rabbets.

Center-drill the ends of 12 pieces of 3/4 in. dowel 6-3/4 in. long, as indicated. These are pilot holes to receive screws driven through the rails and stiles.

Assemble the rails to the stiles and dowels using glue and #8 x 1-3/4 in. flathead wood screws. Note that the bottom rail is attached through the hole that is 2-1/2 in. from the end of each stile. This assures there will be room at the top, under the glass, to insert the bottles in the rack.

The frame for the top is cut from two pieces 17 in. long and two pieces 50 in. long rabbeted as indicated. Cut the ends at 45 degrees to create mitered corners.

Finally, position the two assembled "pedestals" 6 in. in from the ends of the top frame, with the bottle-neck rails facing each other, drill down through the rabbet as detailed, and drill blind holes in the underside of the frame. Matching holes are drilled in the tops of the stiles for the latter and final assembly is completed. Finishing is left to individual preference,

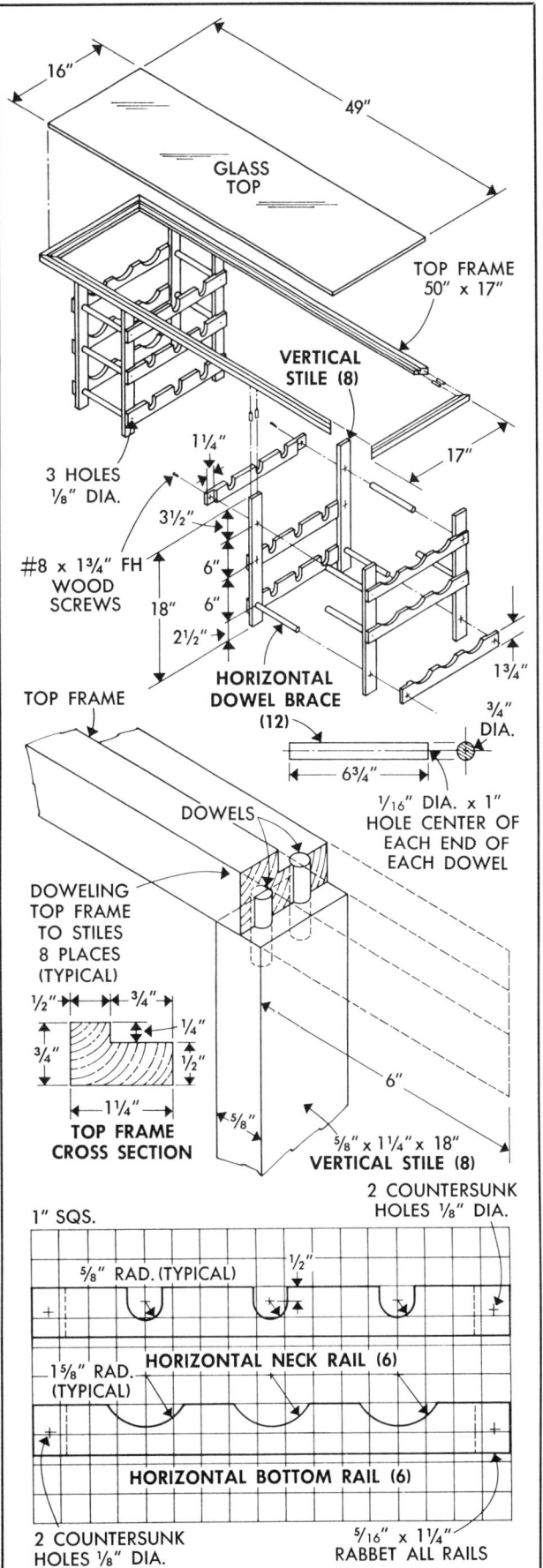

Simple display-top coffee table

Designed originally for a rock hound who wanted a place to display some interesting specimens, this attractive table also serves well as a place to serve coffee. Your interests may not be in rocks or fossils, but many of us have collections we would like to display. For example, the table will make a novel family photo gallery and conversation piece.

Start construction by cutting and assembling a mitered frame of 3/8 x 1 in. stock measuring 40 x 48 in. outside. If stock of different thickness is used, change the leg notches to suit. A panel of 1/4 in. plywood 3/4 in. longer and wider than the inside dimensions of the frame now is cut and attached to the frame so it overlaps 3/8 in. all around. Assemble the aprons, using corrugated fasteners or splines, shape the "wings" for the top, cut the glass rabbets and assemble them with splines. Attach the legs, that can be turned or of square section.

Before cutting the double-strength window glass or unbreakable plastic top, remeasure and check the square of the rabbetted glass holder. A glass cut to fit properly will hide any error. More important, once a glass is cut, trying to "dress" it to fit a slight miscalculation often results in a broken glass and added expense to cut a new piece. Play it safe, remeasure before cutting. Should you already have cut the glass and it doesn't fit, your best solution is to very carefully dress the frame with sandpaper. Take pains to see that this dressing is gradual along the channel and doesn't leave noticeable dips or gouges.

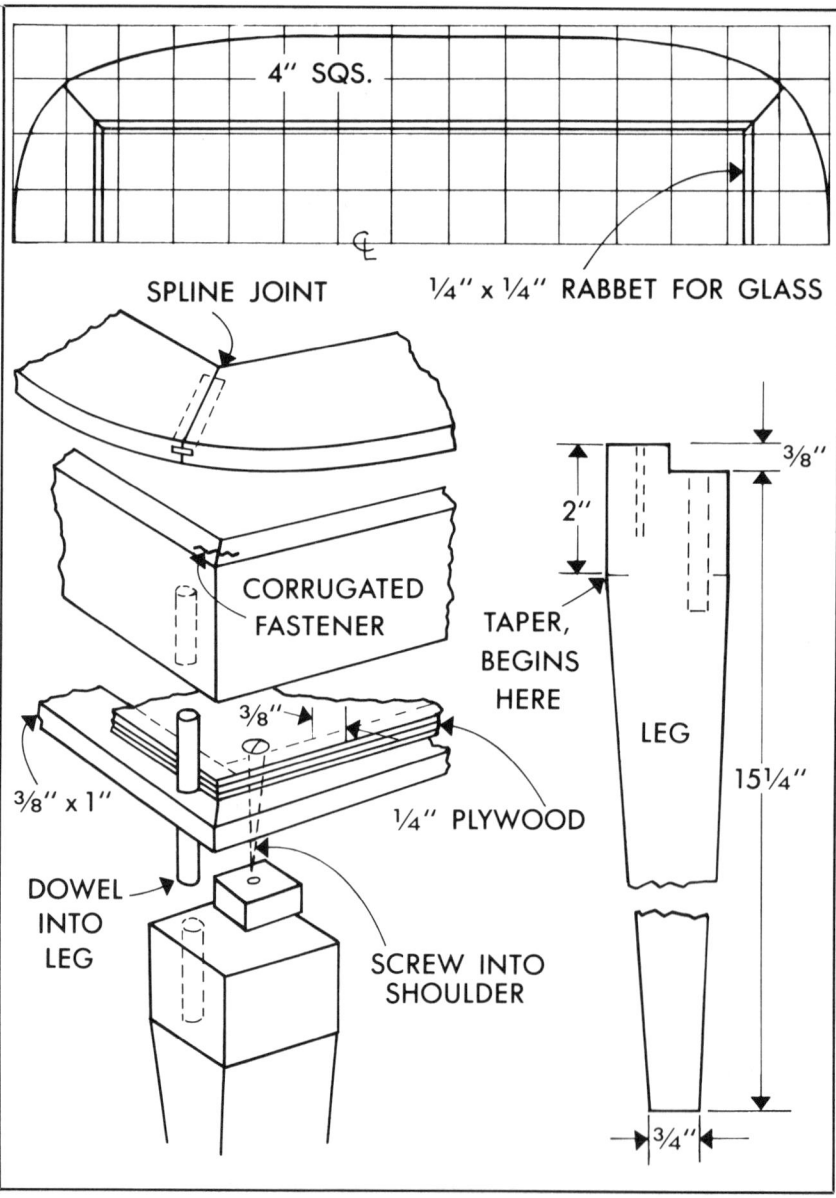

Octagonal display case coffee table

This table's design is Mediterranean, but the broad, shallow display area can be used to house any attractive collection of small items. The original table displays a collection of North American Indian arrowheads and related pieces.

Plywood and dimension lumber are used for all components except the spindles. These can be turned in the shop or purchased.

Use the glass cover (precut to size and shape) as a template for the bottom of the display area and bottom shelf. Outline the octagonal glass on 3/4 in. plywood then mark around three inches outside the first marked area for the final plywood pattern.

Cut the display-area bottom and bottom shelf, then cut 2 x 4 glass supports and all 1 x 4 edge facings as shown in the drawings. Rabbet the glass supports to accept the glass insert without forcing.

Mark all edge facings with the designated 3-1/4 in. carving pattern ("C" and reversed "C"). Rout or carve out this optional decoration.

Attach the glass supports to the plywood with glue and nails, then invert the top assembly. Drill for dowels and attach leg spindles with glue and dowels.

Cut bottom cross braces, foot supports and edge supports ripped to 2-3/4 in. and assemble the bottom. Note that the cross braces are joined with a half-lap. The edge supports are notched to accept the brace ends.

Invert the bottom and attach it in place on the spindles, again using glue and dowels. Attach the feet by the same method.

Turn the entire assembly upright and add the top and bottom edge facings. Sand all surfaces that will be exposed, wipe with a tack-rag and finish. Cover the bottom of the display area with felt, velvet or other suitable material. White sand is an excellent base for seashells, for example. Insert double-strength window glass to complete the project.

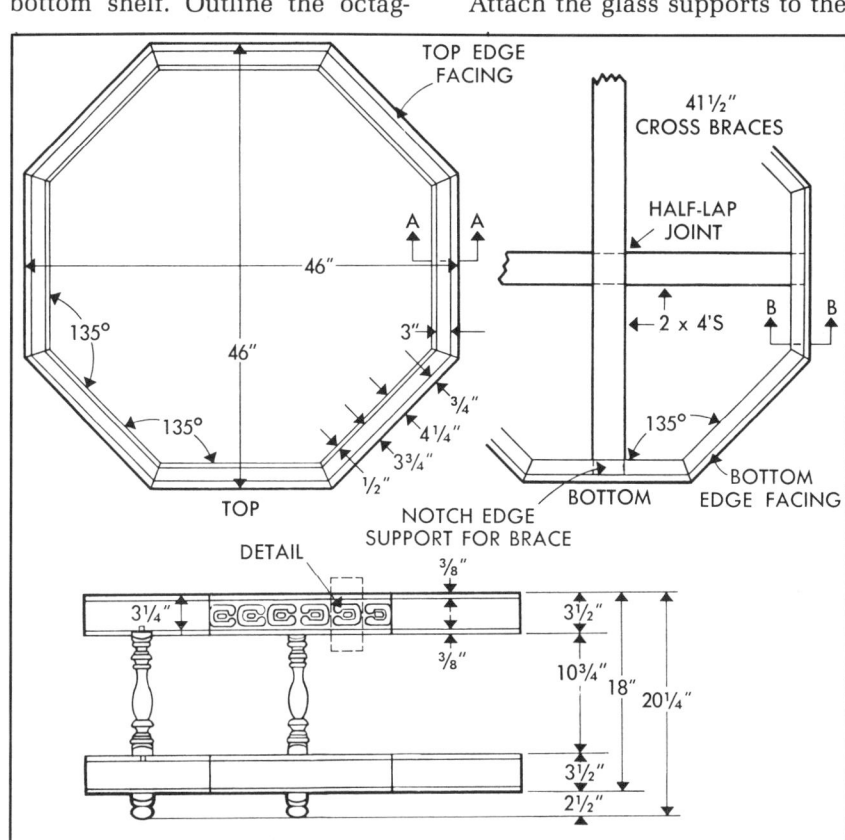

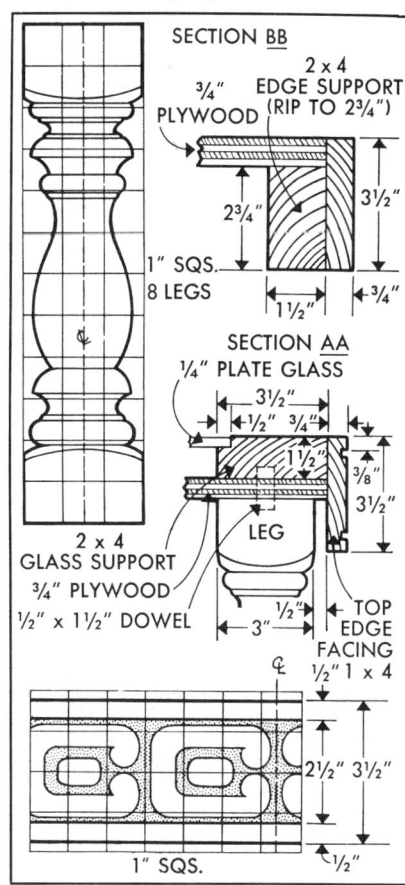

Display coffee table with cabinet

This versatile, space-saving piece of furniture combines the functions of a coffee table, display table, magazine rack and storage cabinet for items such as record albums or tapes.

Oak was used for the table shown, but any hardwood would be suitable. If you can't find stock heavy enough for the top frame (oak truck stakes are one source), you'll have to glue-up blocks from 3/4 in. stock.

Hardwood plywood or veneered particleboard can be used for much of the "case" of the table cabinet, although for the one shown pieces of solid stock were edge-glued to create pieces from which the doors, fronts, back and bottom as well as the top center section were cut.

Cut the various pieces to size as indicated on the drawing, then dowel the back, front and storage compartment sections to the bottom. "Dry-assemble" for fit at this time, but do not glue. Take the assembly apart and cut the 3/4 x 3/4 in. strips that support the backs of the magazine racks and glue and screw them in place on the back and front members as shown.

Next, glue the lower edge of the back to the bottom, clamp and let set overnight.

Glue the compartment ends and front pieces together and to the bottom, and hold with clamps until the glue sets, which again should be at least overnight.

The "backs" of the magazine racks are cut from 1/4 in. particleboard or hardwood-plywood, then glued and bradded to the support strips. Stop strips for the bottoms of the magazine racks are 1/4 x 1/4 x 14-1/2 in. and are glued and nailed to the bottom of each magazine compartment. Note that the strips are positioned 1/2 in. from the ends of the compartments.

Hang the doors, using offset hinges, as used on kitchen-cabinet doors. Keep the lower edges of the doors in line with the lower edges of the front sections of the cabinet.

Cut the four outside framing strips for the tabletop to the sizes given. Note that the short end pieces have rabbets cut the full length on the upper and lower inner edges. The upper rabbet is 1/8 in. deep for the double-strength window glass and 1/4 in. wide. The lower rabbet is 1/4 x 1/4 to accept the 1/4 in. plywood bottom of the top assembly. The bottom runs the full length and width of the top frame, fitting in the rabbets.

Stopped rabbets are cut into the

Attach support strips for magazine rack backs to the front and back boards with screws.

Close dado cuts at ends of cross dividers with cut-to-fit oak pieces.

Peg and glue compartment ends and front pieces to the bottom, clamp to dry.

Fit top to base and fasten together with screws driven through bottom into back and front of frame.

Nail magazine rest pieces to the support strips. Glue and nail magazine stop strips to the bottom ½ in. back from the edge.

Fit and glue the tabletop board into the frame.

upper edges of the long pieces of the top frame, starting 1-1/2 in. from each end and running 7-5/8 in. long to accommodate the glass covers for the display compartments. If you cut the stopped rabbets with a circular saw, it will be necessary to square up the curved ends with a wood chisel.

Glue the four pieces of the frame together, then turn it over and glue the plywood bottom in the rabbets.

Cut and rabbet the pieces for the inner ends of the display compartments, and the shorter pieces that divide the display compartments. Glue them in place and, when the glue has set, turn the top assembly upside down and drive screws through the bottom into the pieces.

Cut filler strips to fit in the rabbets at the ends of the compartment dividers. Alternately, when you cut those pieces, shape them with an overhanging lip to fit into the rabbet.

Set the completed tabletop on the cabinet base and drive four #8 x 1-1/4 in. screws down through the 1/4 in. plywood into the back, and two each of the screws down into the front pieces.

Cut the support strips for inside the center compartment, and glue and screw them into position so the 3/4 in. top fits flush with the top of the frame. Glue the top to the strips.

Magnetic catches are screwed to the underside of the tabletop, with plates on the doors. Install suitable door pulls.

Four "feet" measuring 3/4 x 2 x 2 in. are glued and screwed to the bottom of the cabinet, spaced 1 in. in from the corners.

Stain and finish to suit your taste, then glue pieces of felt, velvet, or some other lining material into the bottoms of the display compartments.

Measure the display compartments, from rabbet to rabbet in each direction and have pieces of double-strength window glass cut. The glass should be slightly loose, so a nail file or similar item can be used to pry up the glass when you want to change displays or clean the glass.

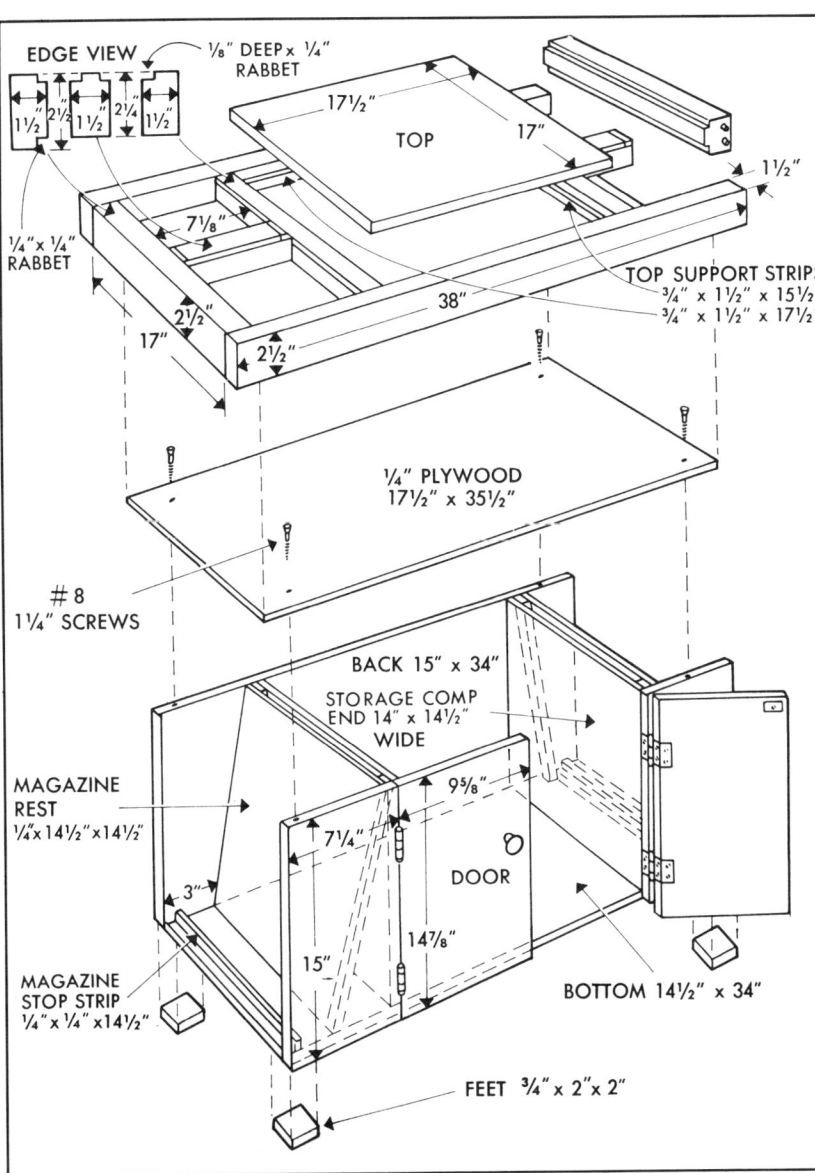

John-boy coffee table

The planks in this coffee table are reminiscent of the ruggedly aged flooring in America's oldest inns, where history was made over cups of coffee and other beverages. The table is easy to build, and the use of readily available or distressed lumber keeps costs at a minimum and adds to authenticity.

Begin work by cutting four lengths of 2 x 6 tongue-and-groove roof decking for the top planks, plus a length of straight 2 x 6 for a lower brace. Rip a 2 x 4 in half to provide end pieces for the top.

Glue and clamp the planks together, keeping their ends precisely aligned. When the glue joining the planks has set, attach the end strips with glue and nails.

Put the tabletop aside and cut six pieces of 2 x 6 decking for the legs. Trim the two bottom pieces to height, then saw the cutouts in the pieces.

Further work on the legs is the same as for the top using tongue-and-groove with edging except that a 2 x 2 is ripped to provide the edge strips.

Bore and counterbore holes to join the top to the legs as shown. Screw the top in place, but don't yet insert the dowel plugs.

The extra length of 2 x 6 that was cut and trimmed with the top planks should be placed between the legs as a stretcher. Glue and screw this crosspiece in position, supporting it so that its bottom edge is even with the top of the leg cutouts.

With rasp and sandpaper, round off all exposed edges and corners. To avoid possible splintering along the joint lines, exercise caution in rounding the narrow trim strips on the edges of the legs.

If you desire a finish similar to that shown in the photographs, now is the time to distress (mar) the wood. Remember that the purpose of distressing is to simulate the wear-and-tear of normal aging, so plan your assault accordingly. Carved initials may add an interesting touch, for example. But remember, they'll be there a long time.

Use chains, a sack of rocks, a hammer and whatever else will render the effects you want. A heated nail or small drill bit can be used to create "worm holes." Some restraint is called for, as you don't want to undo the work you've done.

When you're satisfied with the degree of "aging" inflicted, retighten the screws in the top and reseat any nails that appear to have loosened. Apply glue and insert dowel plugs in the top holes, trim the plugs and sand as necessary. The table is now ready for staining, sealing and finishing.

Solid, sturdy, and reminiscent of Colonial times in early America is this rugged, easily made coffee table.

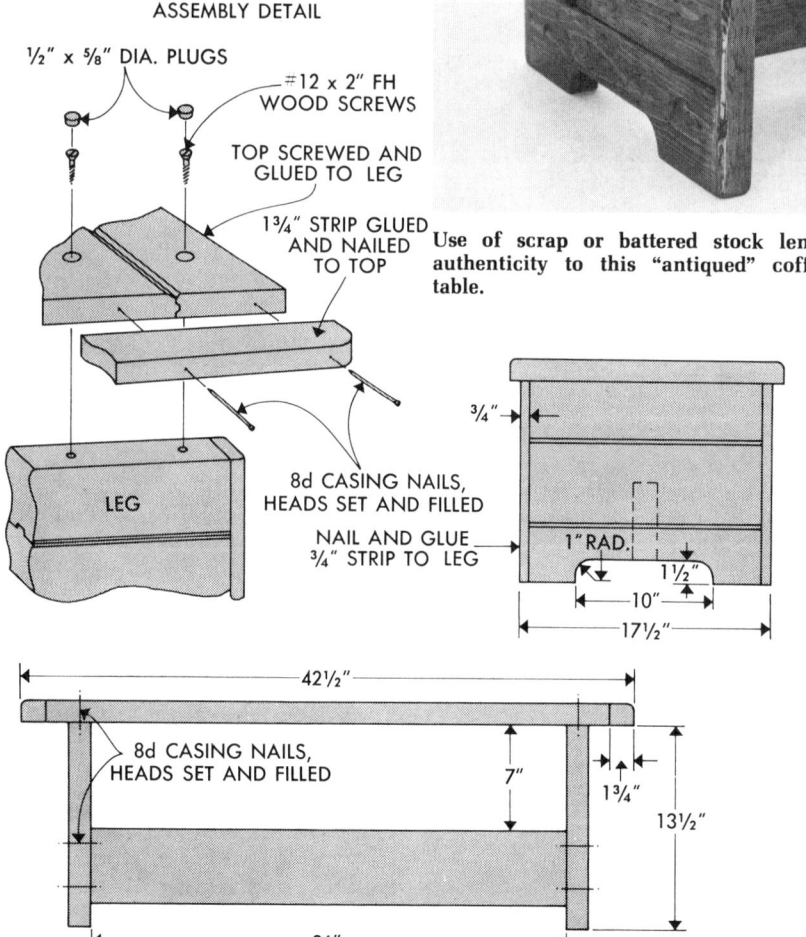

Use of scrap or battered stock lends authenticity to this "antiqued" coffee table.

Burn-finished coffee table

Some table projects can be demanding, time consuming and expensive. Here's one that's easy to build, takes little time and the materials can be found in the scrap piles of most home shops.

The final result is a durable coffee table, built entirely from scrap and stained with fire, for a handsome addition to the den or recreation room.

This one was made from 2 x 4s left over from another project, including a baseboard of plywood recovered from a concrete form. The irregular lengths of the 2 x 4s don't make any difference because that is how they will be cut anyway.

The baseboard can be made from just about any material on hand since its only function is to support the legs and top, and it will be hidden from view in the finished product.

Varying widths of 5/8 in. plywood were used in this one, but a single sheet will work as well. A good idea is the addition of cleats across the base ends, for greater strength.

The dimensions are variable, depending on the size you want. However, in that 2 x 4s differ in size, 1-1/2 x 3-1/2 seasoned, 1-5/8 x 3-5/8 unseasoned, you'll want to adjust dimensions to fit the wood you have on hand.

An alternate method would be to build the top first, then construct the base to fit it.

In this model, the 2 x 4s nest side by side and are removable so that any single piece accidentally damaged may be replaced.

Another method could include attaching the pieces with wood screws from the underside, or for a smoother finished top, glue-assemble in clamps for a laminated look.

Four 11 in. legs are cut from pairs of 2 x 4s, then attached to the corners of the baseboard with screws down through the top. The rails are 2 x 4s which form a tray for the random pieces and strengthen the leg assemblies. Countersunk screws are driven through the rails and into the legs. Add corner brackets as shown to make the leg assemblies more rigid.

Once the random lengths of 2 x 4s are fitted into the tray, you are ready for burning to bring out the grain. Clear lumber was used in this table, but knots may add to the appearance.

"Paint" the flames over the entire surface, remembering the inside of the legs. To determine shading desired and consistency, practice on scrap first.

Guests will want to know the "story" behind this unique coffee table with its burnt wood top.

Burning in the finish can be done before or after assembly depending on whether or not you want the sideboards scorched.

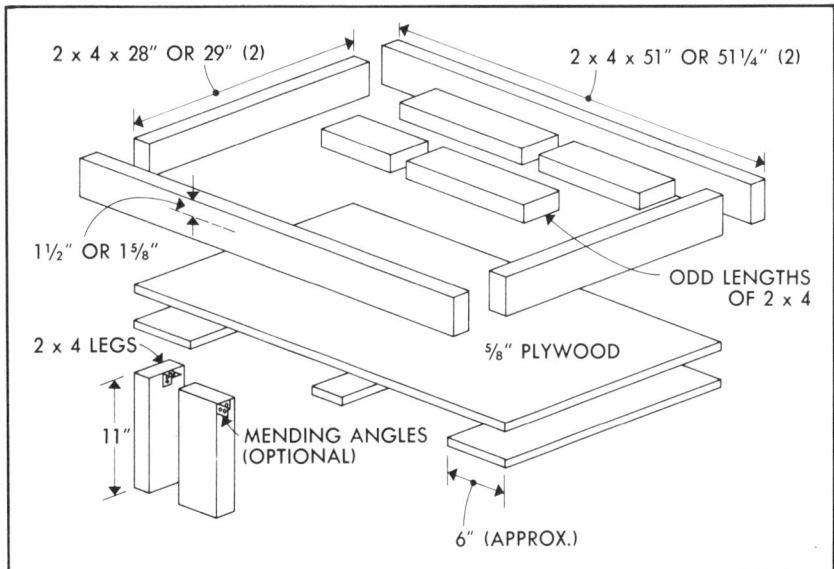

Rugged cedar and pine coffee table

Red cedar and pine were the contrasting woods chosen for the original model of this sturdy coffee table, but maple and walnut, mahogany and basswood, or other combinations would be just as interesting.

The cedar was ripped into strips 5-1/4 in. wide, then glued and screwed to a sheet of 1/2 in. plywood just a bit larger than the finished insert for the top needed to be. The strips are angled 45 degrees.

You can, of course, make the table larger or smaller than the dimensions shown. This insert was trimmed to be 16 x 44-3/4 in. to fit the frame.

The frame was assembled from "old-fashioned" pine 2 x 4s that measure about 1-3/4 x 3-3/4 in. If you use 2 x 4s with the latest dimensions, they will measure just 1-1/2 x 3-1/2 in. Which means that after you cut the rabbets in the frame to accept the 1-1/4 in. cedar/plywood "sandwich," you will need only 1/4 in. spacers to fit between the legs and the underside of the top, rather than the 1/2 in. shown.

Incidentally, the frame was assembled with splined miter joints, then the insert was trimmed to be a snug fit in the frame. The miter joints also can be reinforced with dowels rather than splines, and a contrasting color on the ends of the dowels will create a "rustic" appearance.

The legs are assembled from 2 x 4 stock ripped to the dimensions given. The rabbeted joints take a bit of figuring, as the bottoms of the rabbets are not at right angles. Note that the top rabbets have joints that are 100 degrees, 10 degrees more than a right angle, while the bottom rabbets are 80 degrees, 10 degrees less than a right angle.

Assemble the legs with glue and 1-1/2 in. finishing nails. Countersink the nails and cover the heads with wood putty. Alternately, use wood screws in counterbored holes, then cover the screw heads with wooden plugs.

It's a good idea to use metal or carpet-covered glides on the bottoms of the legs. This would protect the finish on the bottoms of the legs, and make the table easier to move.

Attach the assembled legs to the underside of the tabletop by running wood screws up through counterbored holes as indicated in the drawing. Glue will make the attachment of the legs to the top stronger, but if you want to be able to remove the legs for easy storage or transport, use only the screws.

Finally, sand all surfaces smooth, stain and finish.

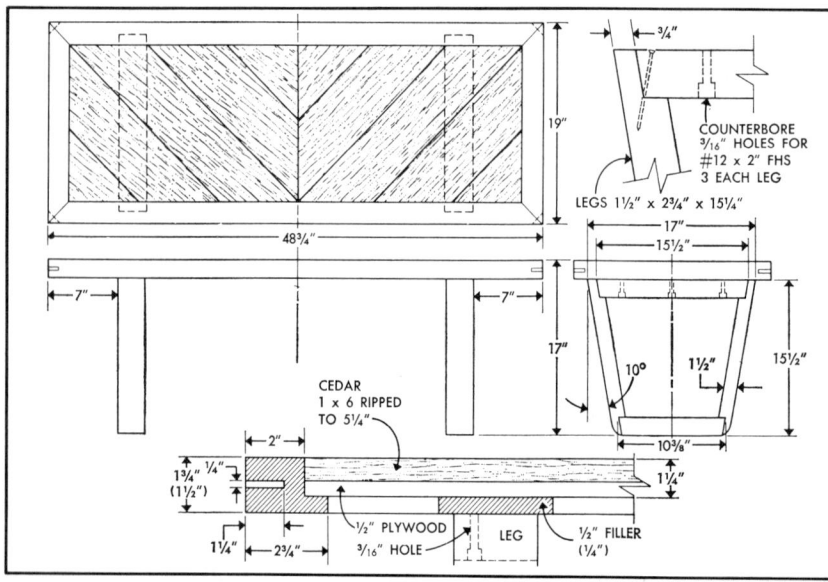

Ceramic tile, spanish style coffee table

This handsomely solid coffee table combines ceramic tile and a massive wood frame for a bright and colorful contemporary Spanish look. It's easy to build and you can choose whatever tile best fits your present decor.

Clear grade Douglas fir 4 x 4s were used for the original frame, but if some other type of wood is a favorite of yours use it.

The actual dimensions of a 4 x 4 are 3-1/2 x 3-1/2 in., and the boards for this table need to be planed, or sawed and smoothed, to 3 x 3 in. size. After reducing the wood to the correct finished dimensions, begin with the assembly of the tabletop. Cut two 6 ft. boards and twelve 9 in. pieces as shown, making sure they are properly aligned. Next glue the long boards to these "stacks" to form a rectangle.

Around the inside of this assembly, glue and screw 2 x 2 support cleats for the tabletop. To determine the exact placement of the cleats, measure the thickness of the ceramic tile and add it to that of the 3/4 in. plywood top. The cleats should be placed that combined distance from the top of the table. Glue and nail the plywood top to the cleats, and you're ready to add the table legs.

Attach the 3 x 3 cross supports to each end with glue and then add the table legs. Now drive three wood screws at the positions indicated. The screw holes are counterbored about 1 in. deep with a 3/4 in. diameter hole drilled to accept a wooden plug. Sand all surfaces smooth and flush.

Stain and finish the wood to suit your taste. The original was first stained and then coated with a clear plastic sealer.

The top is finished by spreading a thin layer of tile adhesive on the plywood and spacing the tiles evenly across the top. After the tile adhesive has set, fill the gaps between the tile with grout. When the grout has dried, wipe off "slopovers" with a wet towel and allow grout to cure.

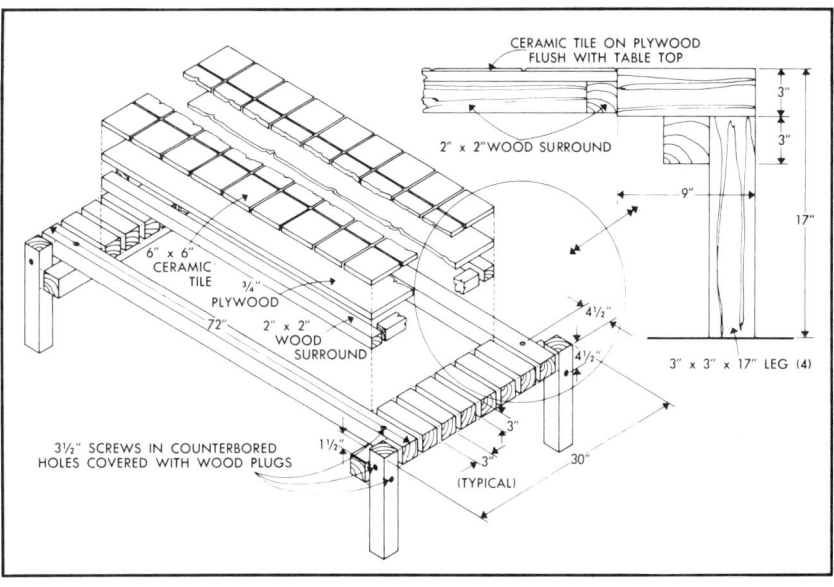

Colonial style table with modern tile top

With colonial keyed-mortise-and-tenon joints and a modern tiled top, this coffee table covers a wide span of time and will fit well into most informal and simple settings.

Construction of the table is relatively simple and with a little effort it can be built with hand tools. If this is necessary, the lumber dealer could make the cuts required for the 1/4 in. lip or frame for the tile, or the molding shown could be one of the standard shapes found at most lumber dealers. The miter cuts at the table corners can be made using a homemade miter box constructed from scrap lumber.

The ends of the table, as shown in the drawings, are made from 2 in. nominal clear white pine milled to 1-3/4 in. finished. It is unlikely that this can be obtained in stock in 17 in. widths, but will have to be made from three pieces glued together. If the surfaces to be joined are smooth and well prepared, the joints are made without splines. However, if possible, it would be preferable to use splines for the joint. It might be noted that before dimensions are finalized, the tile of the top should be on hand and a preliminary fitting made to eliminate the task of cutting tile. Be sure to allow about 1/4 in. between all tiles for grouting. Even if random size tile or chips are selected, the layout of the top should be checked. The table as pictured is 56 in. long but this length is subject to change to meet the builder's needs. Finish is again the craftsman's choice, and in this case, was an oil stain and multiple coatings of a resin-based finish, rubbed to give a semi-dull luster.

One important consideration in the construction and finishing of the table is installation of the tile. The wood should be stained and at least one coat of finish applied before placing and grouting the tile. The white grout is easily discolored by the stain, but the grout can be removed easily from the partially finished wood edging.

MATERIALS LIST

Top, 3/4 in. plywood, 18" x 54" (1)

Ends, 2" x 6" x 18" (nominal) clear pine (6)

Spreader, 1-1/4" x 2-1/2" x 60", clear pine (1)

Inside rail, 1" x 1-1/2" x 54", pine (2)

Molding, 1" x 1-1/2" x 60", pine (2)

Top Edging, 1" x 1-1/2" x 60", pine (2)

Wedges, 1/4" x 1-1/2" x 6", pine (2)

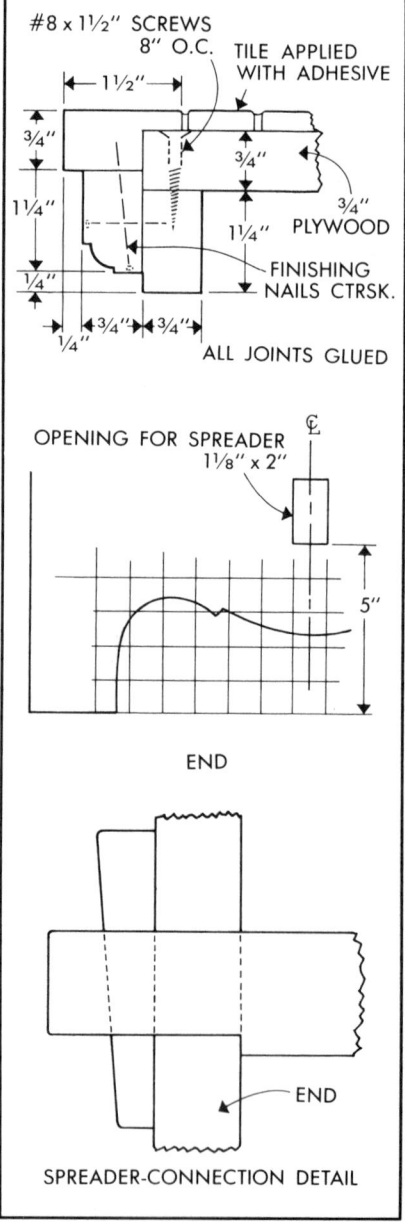

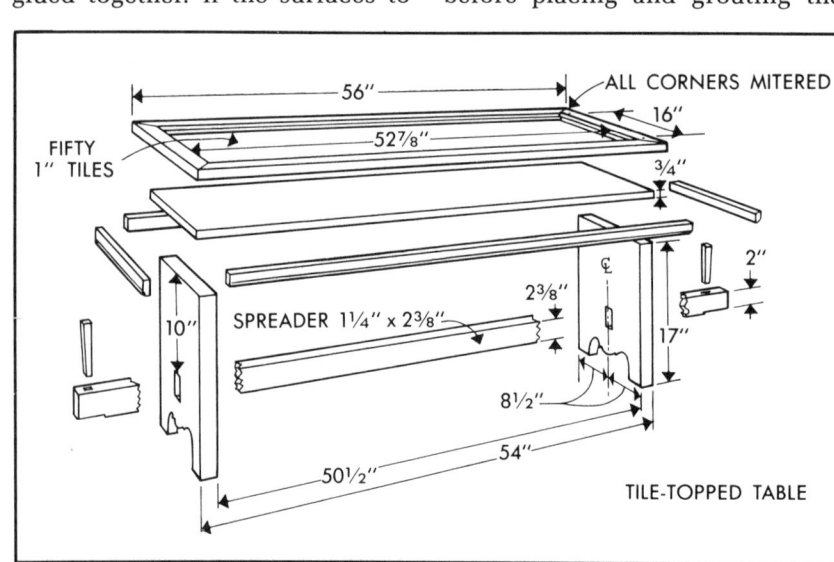

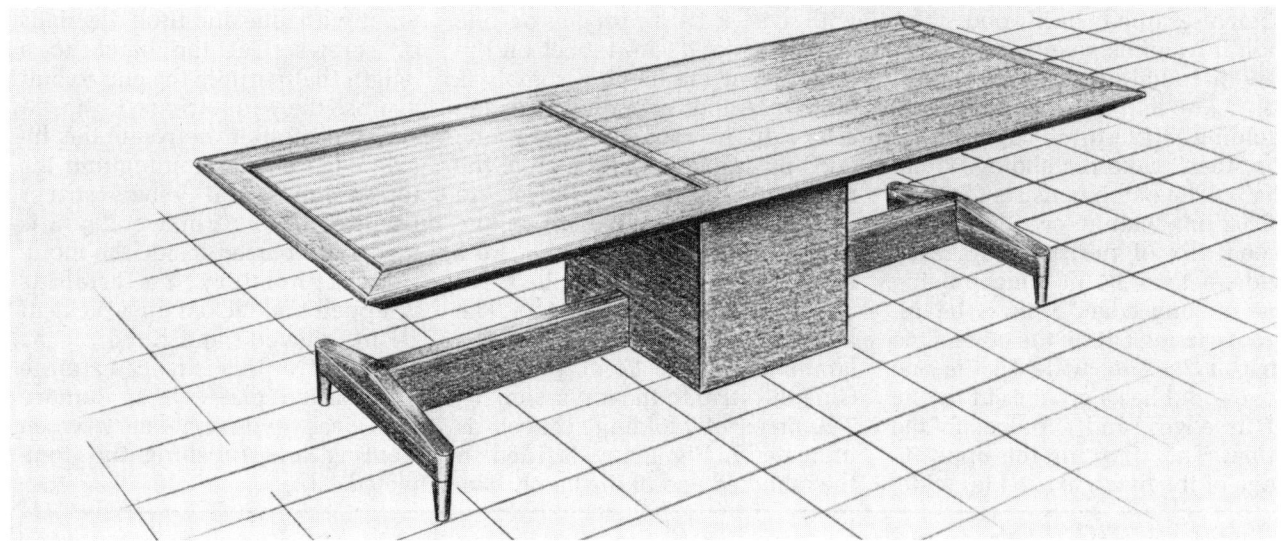

Hide-away wine cabinet coffee table

Intriguing as well as attractive is the design of this clever coffee table. It has a hidden storage compartment in the base that is reached by sliding back a "hatch" assembled from tongue-and-groove strips of hardwood. When the hatch is pulled back it reveals a surface covered with white burn- and alcohol-resistant plastic laminate, on which food and beverages can be served. The laminate makes an easy-to-clean surface, as does the polished glass recessed into the other end of the tabletop. Under the glass is a rectangle of plywood on which might be mounted a piece of upholstery material to match that used on the chair or divan in front of which the table will be placed. Changing the upholstery material will give the table an entirely new look, as is the case with the slip-on sheathes used on the chair or divan.

Construction of the table is not difficult, but there are quite a number of pieces to be cut and fitted. This means close attention to dimensions, and accurate cutting of miters and corners. Start construction by making the base, Fig. 1, that consists of the notched longitudinal piece, the two cross members and the five legs, all hardwood solid stock.

The storage compartment, Figs. 1 and 3, is next. All but the glue blocks are cut from 3/4 in. hardwood plywood. The two side panels, Fig. 3, are the same size, and the end panels are a matching pair, except that one end panel has a dado cut in it to accept the glass-and-cup rack. The vertical edges of the four pieces are mitered at 45 degree angles. On the inside lower edge of each of the four pieces cut a 5/8 x 3/4 in. rabbet. A 3/4 x 1-5/8 in. notch is cut in the lower edge of the two end panels to accept the longitudinal member of the base. On the outside upper edge of each piece cut a 3/8 x 1-1/16 in. rabbet. Two pieces of the 3/4 in. hardwood plywood are cut 5-3/16 x 11-3/4 in. to make the bottom. An opening 1-5/8 in. wide is left between the two pieces to accommodate the longitudinal of the base. Use glue, plus two screws driven through each end panel into the longitudinal to fasten the base and storage compartment together. A glue block now is glued and screwed on the centerline of the outside of each end panel, its upper edge flush with the lower edge of the rabbet.

The tabletop frame, Fig. 2, is next. It is cut from 3/4 x 1-5/8 in. hardwood strips, with the wider dimension horizontal. Two crosspieces are fitted in the frame, being spaced 5-5/8 in. on each side of center to produce an opening 11-1/4 in. wide. Tenons 1/2 x 1/2 in. are cut on the ends of these pieces to fit notches in the frame sides. The length of the crosspieces is determined by measuring between the sides of the assembled frame. A rabbet 3/8 in. deep and 1/2 in. wide is cut in three sides of the assembled frame, as indicated. In the end member of the frame, the one not rabbeted, cut a notch 3/4 x 6 in. for a hand grip. This notch permits grasping the edge of the hatch assembly to pull it out. Over the assembled frame is fitted a piece of 1/4 in. plywood measuring 17 x 56-1/2 in. The end of the plywood is positioned flush with the end of the frame not rabbeted, and allowed to project 1/2 in. beyond the frame at the other end. It also projects 1/2 in. at each side. Mark on the plywood the 11-1/4 x 12-3/4 in. opening between the crosspieces of the frame, and cut this opening in the plywood. Glue and brad the plywood to the frame. Now, cut a piece of 1/16 in. plastic laminate 17 x 34-1/4 in. Place it on the plywood as indicated, Fig. 2, and mark the opening. Cut out the opening then cement the laminate to the plywood with contact adhesive. Attach the top assembly to the storage compartment by driving screws up through the glue blocks into the crosspieces of the top frame. Also use glue on contacting surfaces.

The edge molding for the top is next. On three sides the molding is shaped as in Fig. 2. Use clear, straight-grained hardwood. The molding can be shaped on a table saw or radial arm saw as all surfaces are flat. Fit and miter the molding to the three edges of the top, then make the sliding hatch, Fig. 1. The hatch consists of strips of 1/2 in. walnut or other hardwood. Six of the strips are 2-1/4 wide, a 1/4 x 1/4 in. tongue being cut on one edge, a 1/4 x 1/4 in. groove being cut on the other. One strip is 2-1/2 in. wide—it fits one edge—and has a groove cut in one of its edges, and a rabbet in the other. The strip for the opposite edge of the hatch is 2-3/4 in. wide, with a 1/4 x 1/4 in. tongue on one edge, a 1/4 x 1/2 in. rabbet on the other. After the hatch assembly is glued, clamped and allowed to set, a 1/4 x 1/2 in. rabbet is cut on one end, as indicated, to match the rabbets on the other two edges. A 1 in. strip now is cut from the square end of the 35 in. long hatch. The strip is drilled for dowels, Fig. 2, as is the top. The holes in the top go through the laminate and the 1/4 in. plywood. Glue the strip to the top assembly.

A piece of molding, shaped as indicated in Fig. 1, now is fitted on the rabbeted end of the hatch. Fasten it with glue and finishing nails or screws. Cut the hatch to a length that permits the end to butt against the 1 in. strip, with just a slight clearance between the inside edge of the molding and the top assembly. The U-shape spacer frame of 5/16 x 1/2 in. wood now is made and placed inside the molding. Upholstery material is wrapped and tacked on a piece of 1/4 in. plywood and fitted on the spacer. Over this is placed a piece of polished plate glass. Remove the glass and upholstery when staining and finishing the completed table.

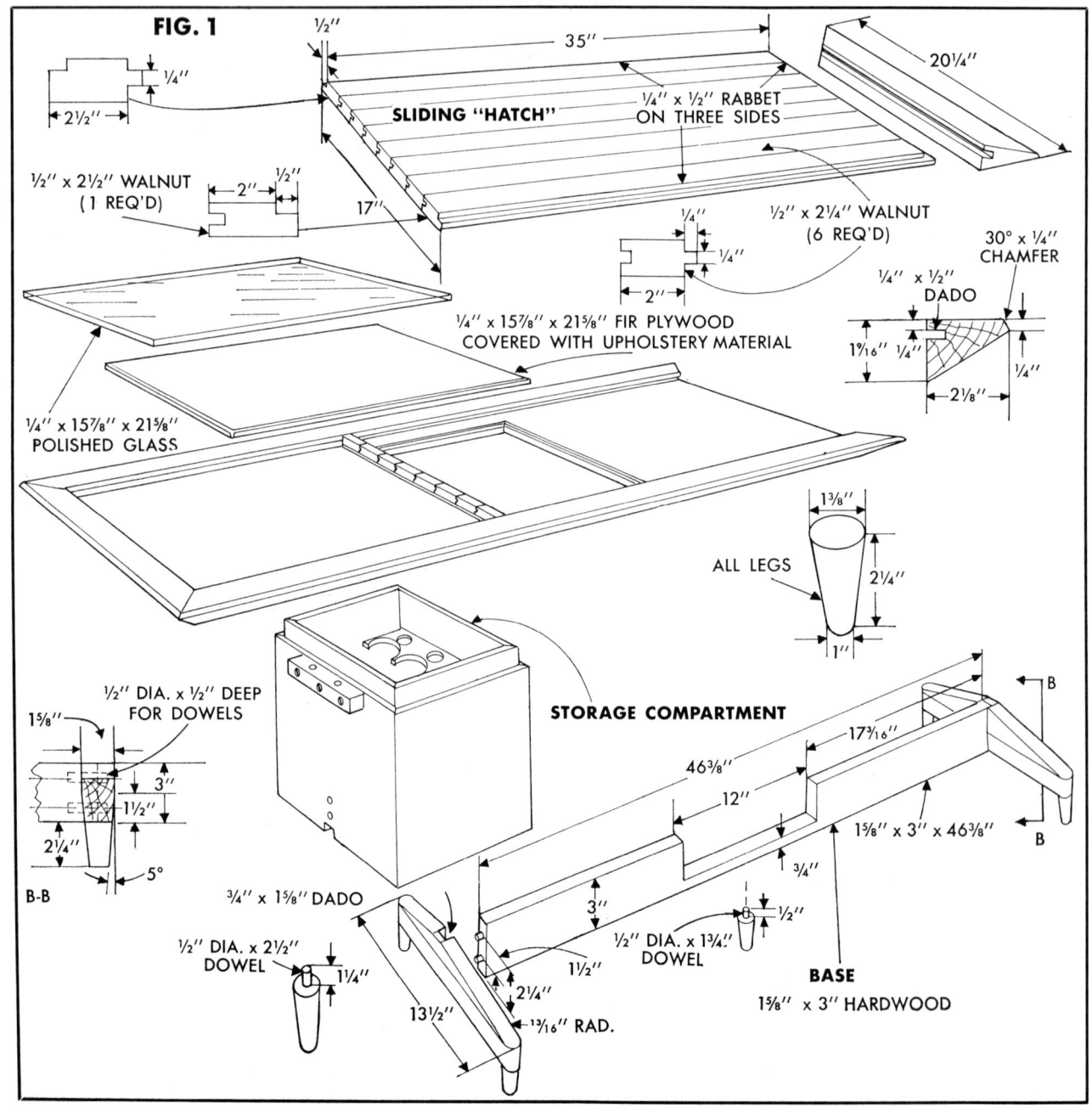

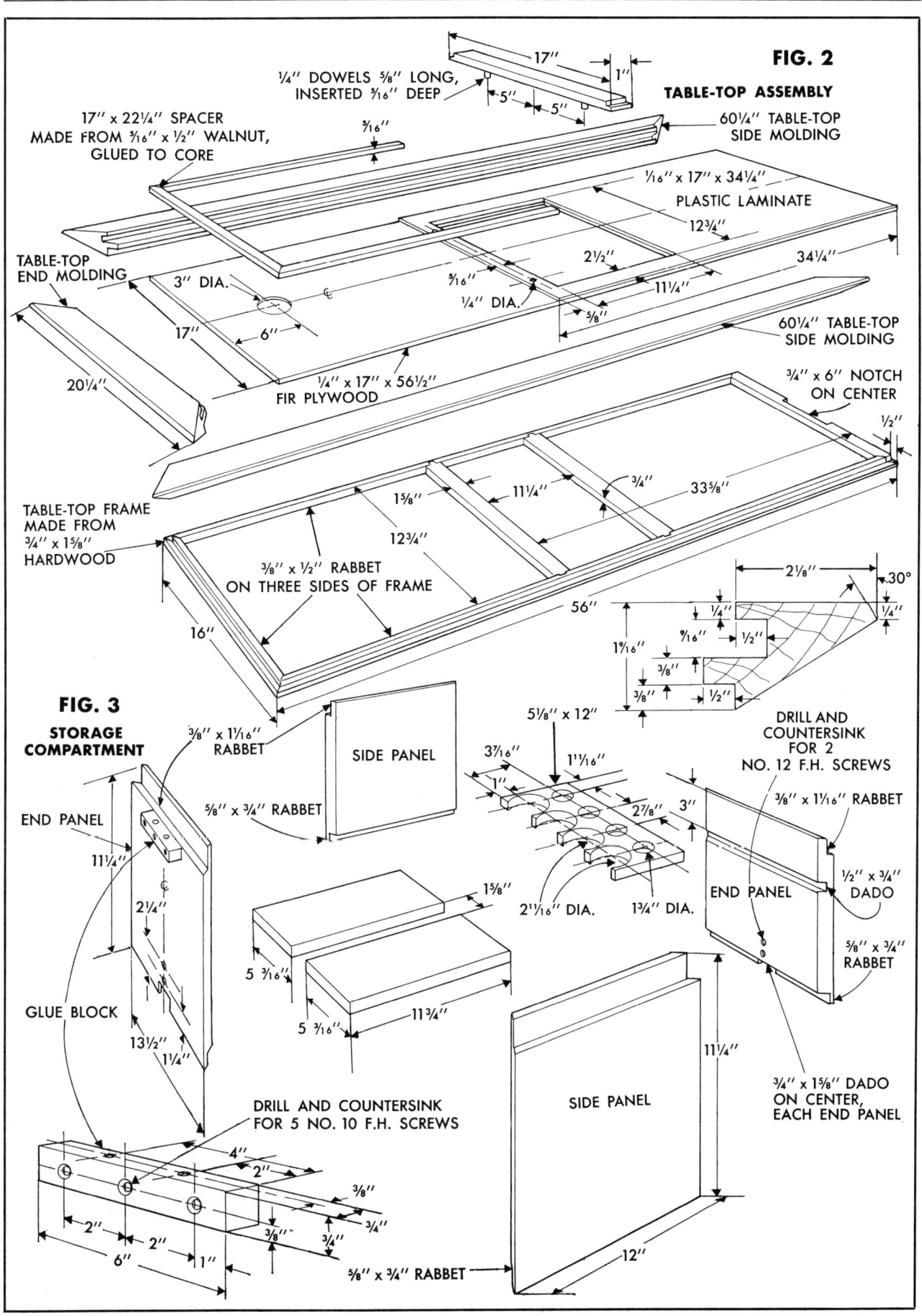

Danish modern coffee table

The key to the graceful elegance of this Danish modern design is the absence of sharp edges with all the lines rounded, tapering and all joints joined smoothly together.

Only a few board feet of hardwood, like the walnut used in the original shown here, are required to make this attractive table. Construction is quite simple, mortise and tenon joints being used between the stretchers and legs. The tenons are cut on the stretchers before they are sawed to shape, so a table or radial arm saw can be used for the job. The tenons are cut in the legs by drilling a row of 1/2 in. holes then cutting out the wood between with a wood chisel.

Legs for the original model were turned from stock 1-3/4 in. sq. and 14 in. long. By carefully centering the stock in the lathe it was possible to produce flats 3/4 in. wide on the upper 4-1/2 in. of the legs. If you have no lathe, purchased tapered legs could be used. Flats would have to be planed and filed to permit a close joint between the legs and ends of the stretchers.

The tabletop is made by edge-gluing strips of stock then sanding the ends round as shown. The side pieces for the top are cut from 1/2 in. stock, roughed to shape, then glued in place. When the glue has set the side pieces are shaped and faired to match the ends of the tabletop.

Note that the short cross members between the legs also require a mortise and tenon joint. The ends of both these members and the stretchers should be cut accurately and the flats on the legs should be parallel to the axis of the legs so that all joints are tight, and the legs all are positioned vertically against the top. Glue is used for all joints. Only four screws are required and they are driven up through counterbored holes in the end cross members into the top to hold it.

Finishing of the wood is what will give your table that professional look. Sand all surfaces well, apply stain and sealer, then at least one good coat of varnish or shellac.

Tenons are cut on stretchers before they are cut to shape, which permits using circular saw for job. Bandsaw or jig saw then is used to cut them to shape.

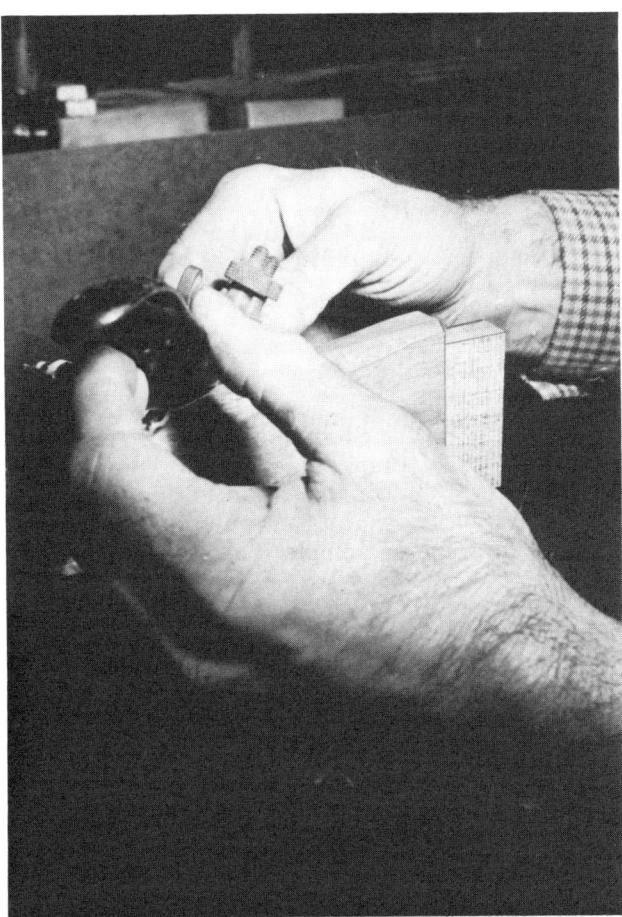

Spokeshave is handy tool for rounding edges of stretchers, but regular plane plus a rasp and sandpaper will do as well. Rounded edges run clear to end.

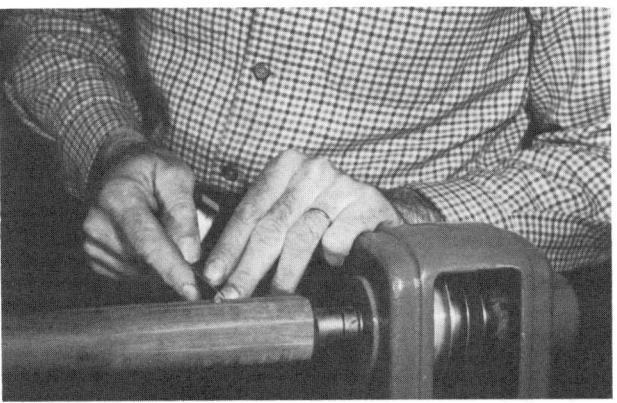

Legs are turned from stock 1¾ in. sq. and 14 in. long. Center stock accurately so that ¾ in. wide flats are left on the upper ends of the legs as shown.

Completely sand and round off ends of tabletop before attaching side members. Latter are then sanded and shaped to fair into ends of top as on completed table.

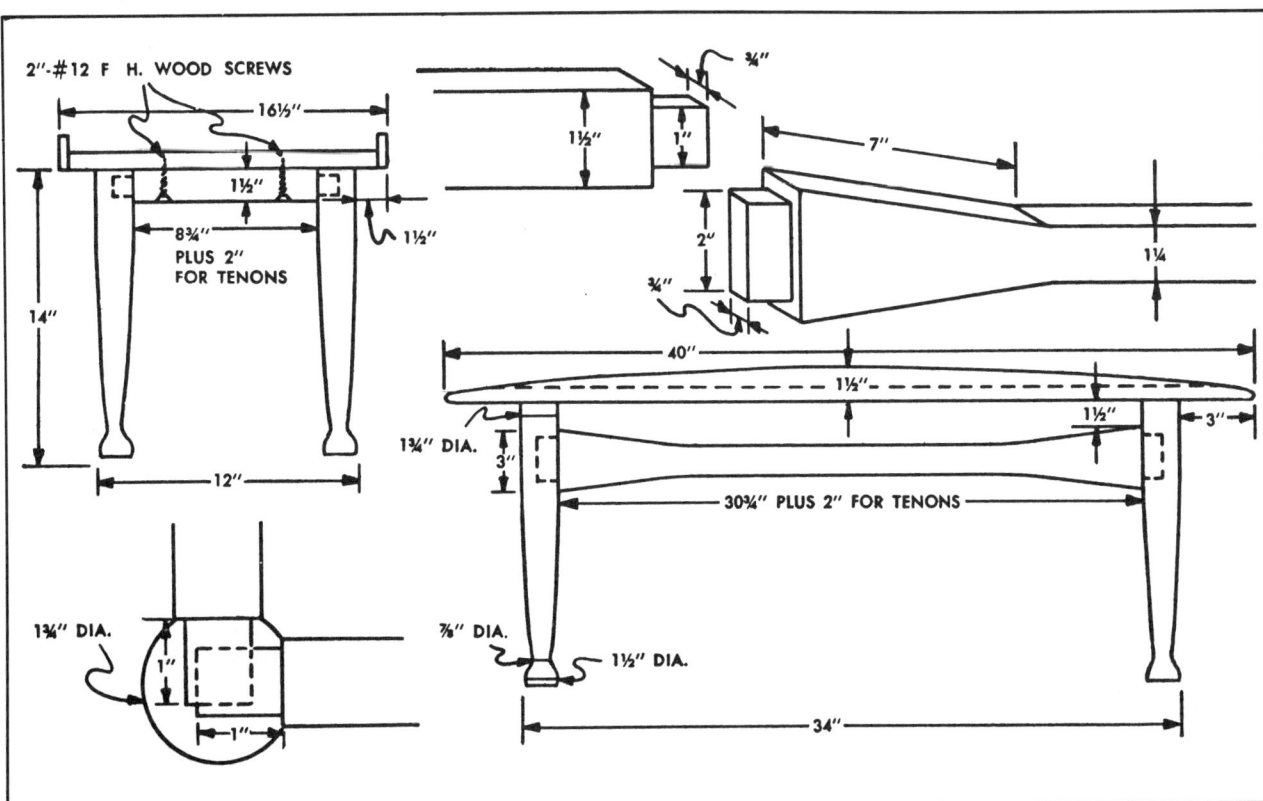

Quick-and-easy coffee table

Simple design plus ready-made tapered brass legs give a degree of sophistication to this coffee table that takes only a few hours to assemble. The table is exceptionally strong and in an emergency can be used as a bench seat.

The tabletop is a piece of 3/4 in. fir plywood reinforced with 1 x 2 strips glued and screwed along the edges on the underside. Measure and miter the strips to come flush with the edges of the plywood. Drill and countersink for the wood screws through the strips about every 8 to 10 in. Sand off any break-through splinters from drilling. Spread glue uniformly over both contacting surfaces and use clamps to hold the strips while driving the screws. Remove the clamps and wipe away excess glue with a damp cloth.

Edging strips, added next, should be close-grained hardwood, 1/4 or 3/8 in. thick. Their width should be 1/16 in. greater than the combined thickness of the plywood top and the reinforcing strips if 1/16 in. plastic laminate is to be used for covering the top. For other materials, such as mosaic tiles or thicker laminates, allow for the required thickness of installing them.

The edging strips can be cut with a molding head in a table saw or shaped by hand with a plane, rasp and sandpaper. Cut the miters accurately on the edging strips. Countersink all nails and fill the holes with wood putty. Screw on the leg plates to the underside of the top, then turn in the legs. Stain and sand the edging strips, then coat with a clear, flat varnish.

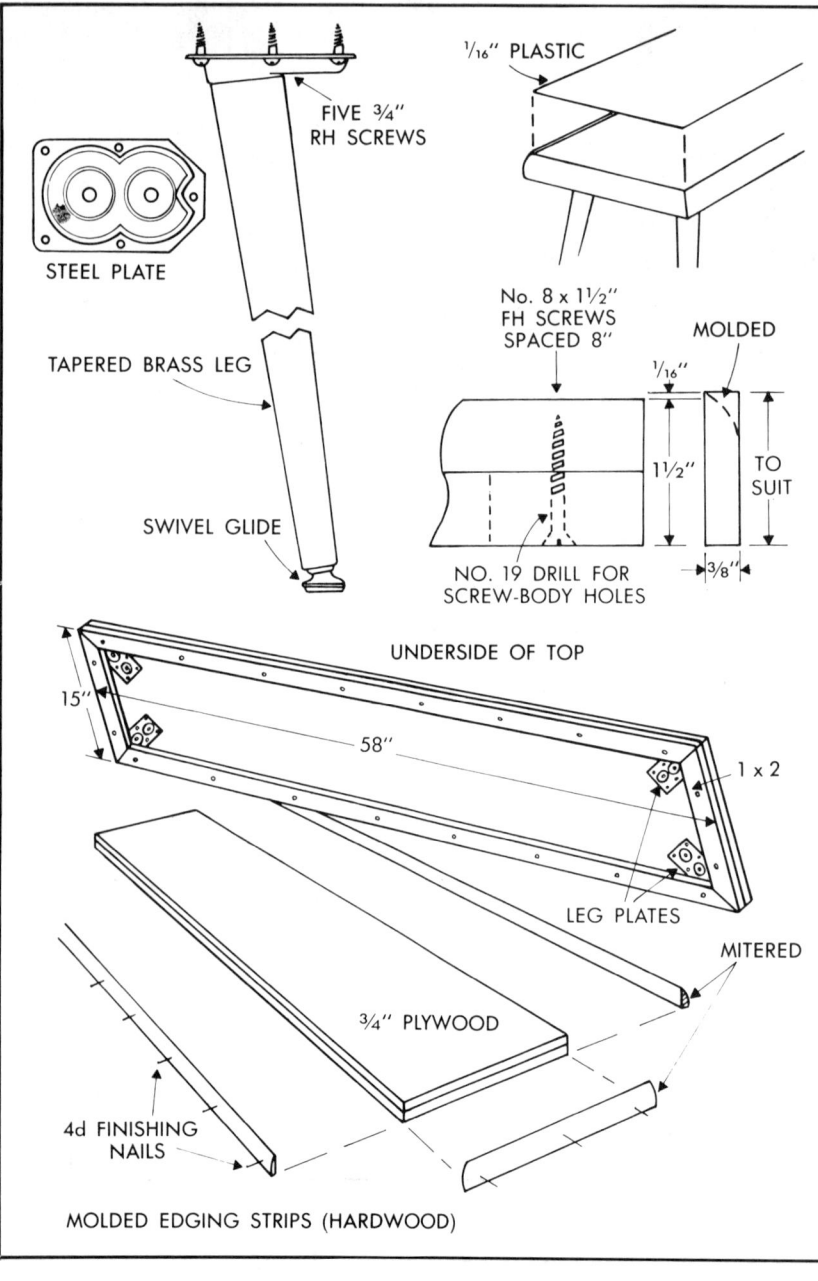

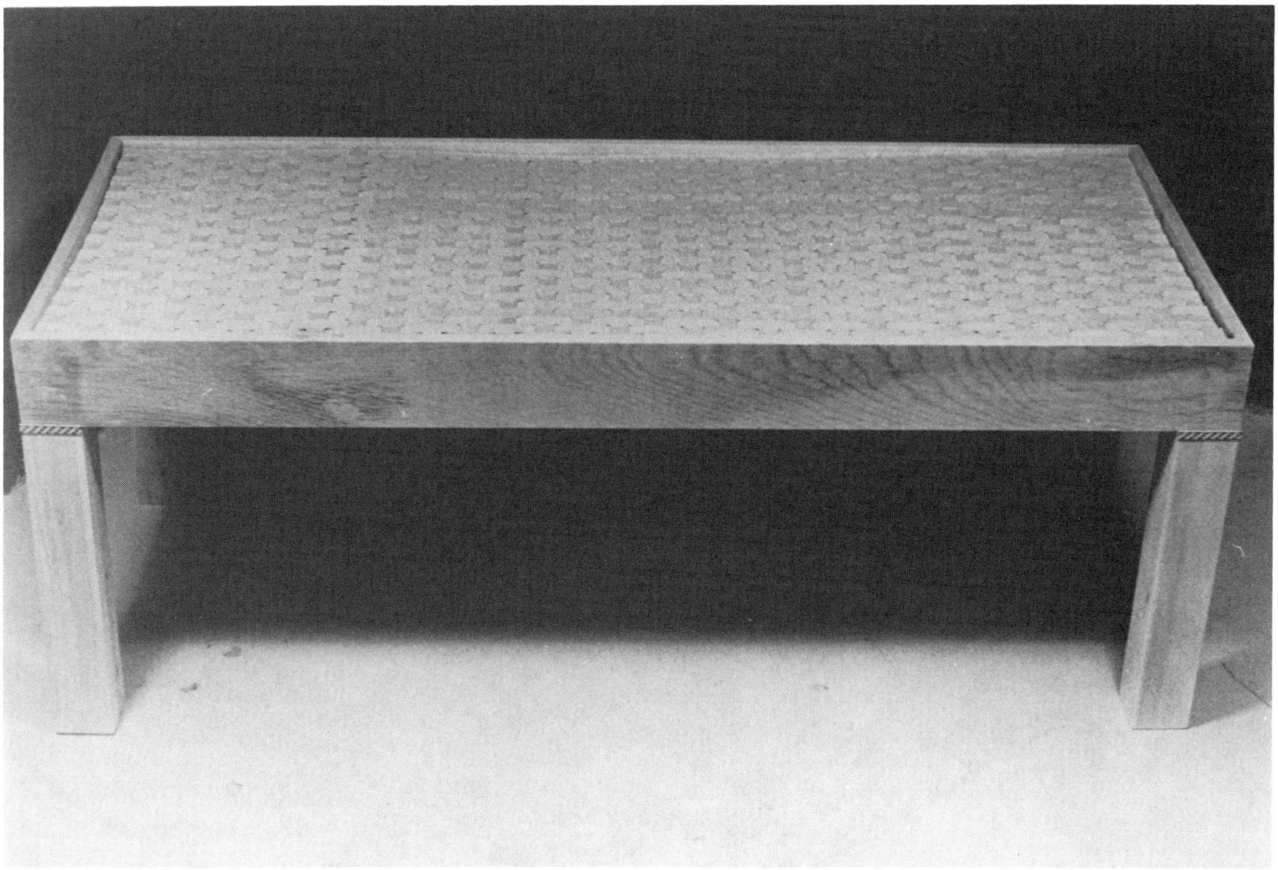

Basket weave-top coffee table

Here's a unique coffee table that's sure to please those who enjoy woven designs. This one was made with softwood, but you may want to use a hardwood. Wider stock could also be used for the legs and rails.

Begin by ripping clear 1 in. stock (3/4 in. net) to 1/32 in. for the top. Rip forty-two strips slightly longer than the desired top length. The shorter crosspieces are sixteen long strips cut in half.

Make the top by squaring the first strip with the end crosspiece. Now, using glue and clothespins, secure the strips to the crosspiece, alternating the strips from top to bottom on the piece. Next, begin weaving the short crosspieces through the strips. The crosspieces are spaced about 2-1/4 in. apart. When you reach the desired length, glue the last crosspiece to the strips. When dry, trim the waste from the top.

Check the top's dimensions, then cut and miter the rails to fit these dimensions. Glue and nail the rails together. Rabbet two sides of each leg 3/4 x 3-1/4 in. wide. Attach the legs to the rails with glue and countersunk screws. Lastly, glue and nail into position the 1 x 2s that help support the top. Attach the supports flush with the top of the legs. Cover the joints between the legs and rails with decorative inlay strips.

Fill all nail and screw holes and stain the table frame and top. The model shown had a clear finish on the frame only, but you may want to finish the top too. The top is protected with a piece of glass cut to fit the inside of the frame.

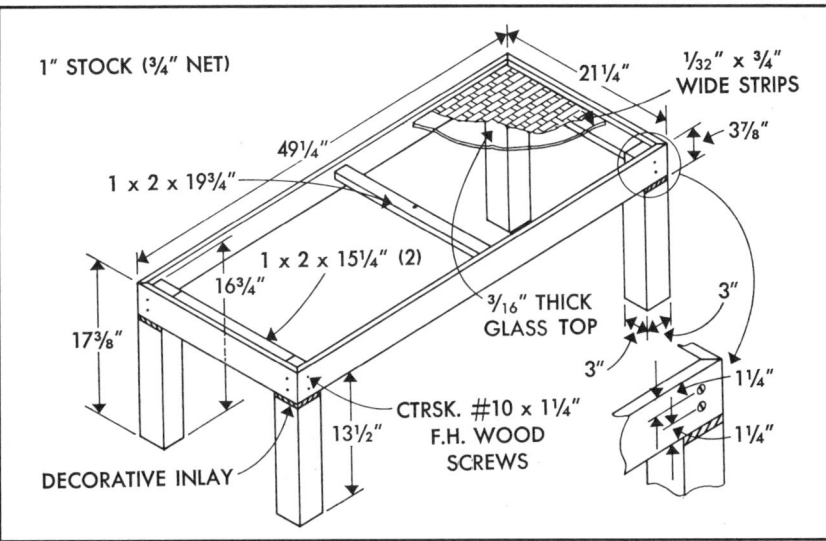

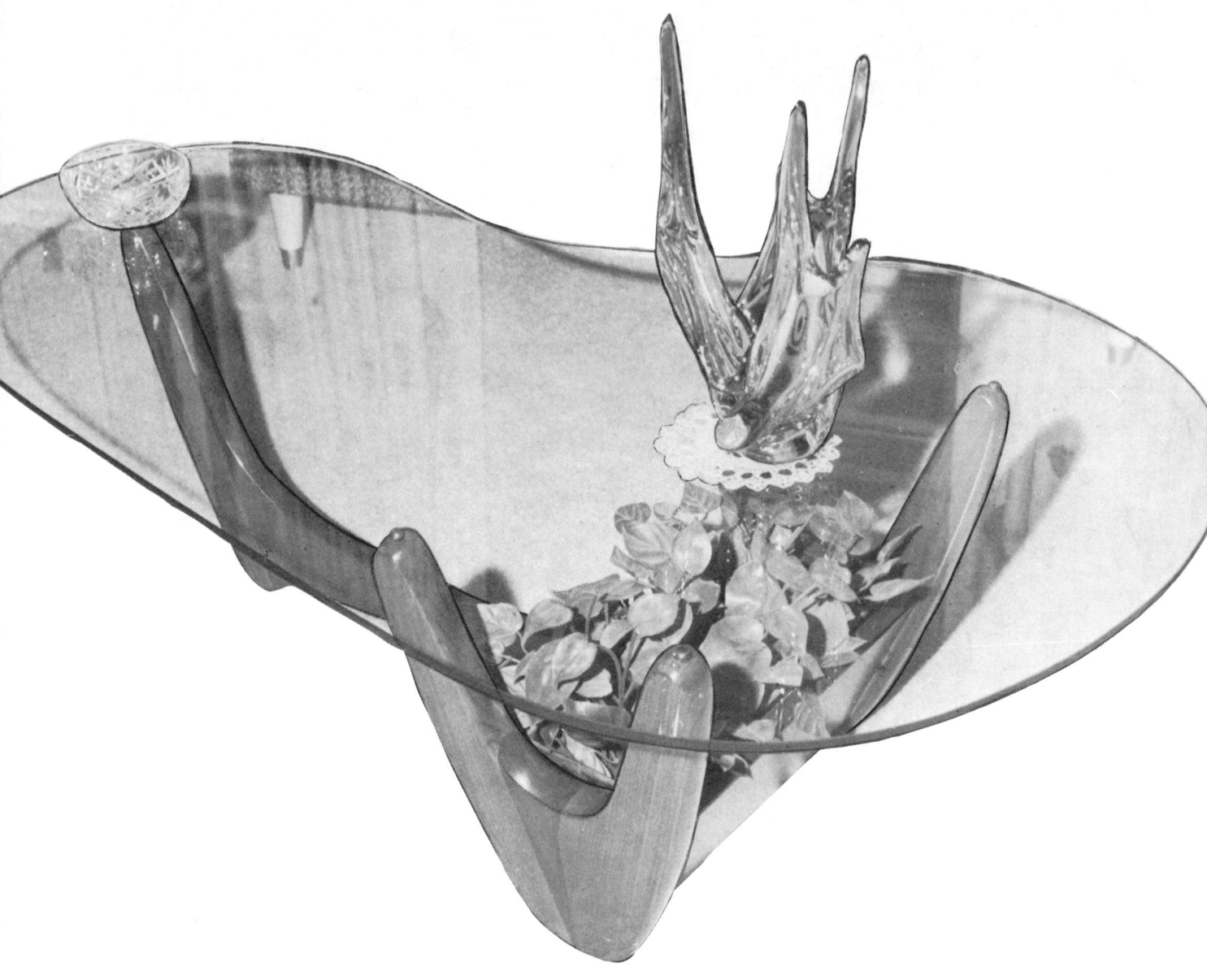

Sculptured, glass-top coffee table

Unusual and interesting, this sculptured base, glass-top table will highlight any living room or den. Its planter box may be filled with houseplants, artificial flowers or ivy, colored rocks, or any number of other attractive items.

Using the diagram, make full-size patterns of the base parts. Glue and dowel two pieces of 1-1/4 in. stock as indicated for each planter end. Follow closely the grain directions indicated. After the glue has dried, clamp the two end pieces together for accuracy when rough-cutting. Finish shaping to final form with rasp and sandpaper. Cut the horizontal centerpiece and third leg from 1-1/4 in. stock, join with glue and dowels, then shape and bring to a smooth finish with rasp and sandpaper. Use 3/4 in. stock for the planter box sides and bottom.

Assemble the box, using glue and dowels at all joints. Add the horizontal centerpiece, then complete with any desired finish. Cap each upright point with a felt pad or rubber-head nail to cushion the glass top. A layer of Styrofoam may be glued in the planter box to hold artificial flower stems, etc.

Use 7/16 in. plate glass for the tabletop. Provide your local glass dealer with a full-size pattern of the kidney shape and he will be able to cut the glass and smooth the edges as needed.

To complete the table, merely lay the glass top on the cushion points, relying on its own weight to hold it in place.

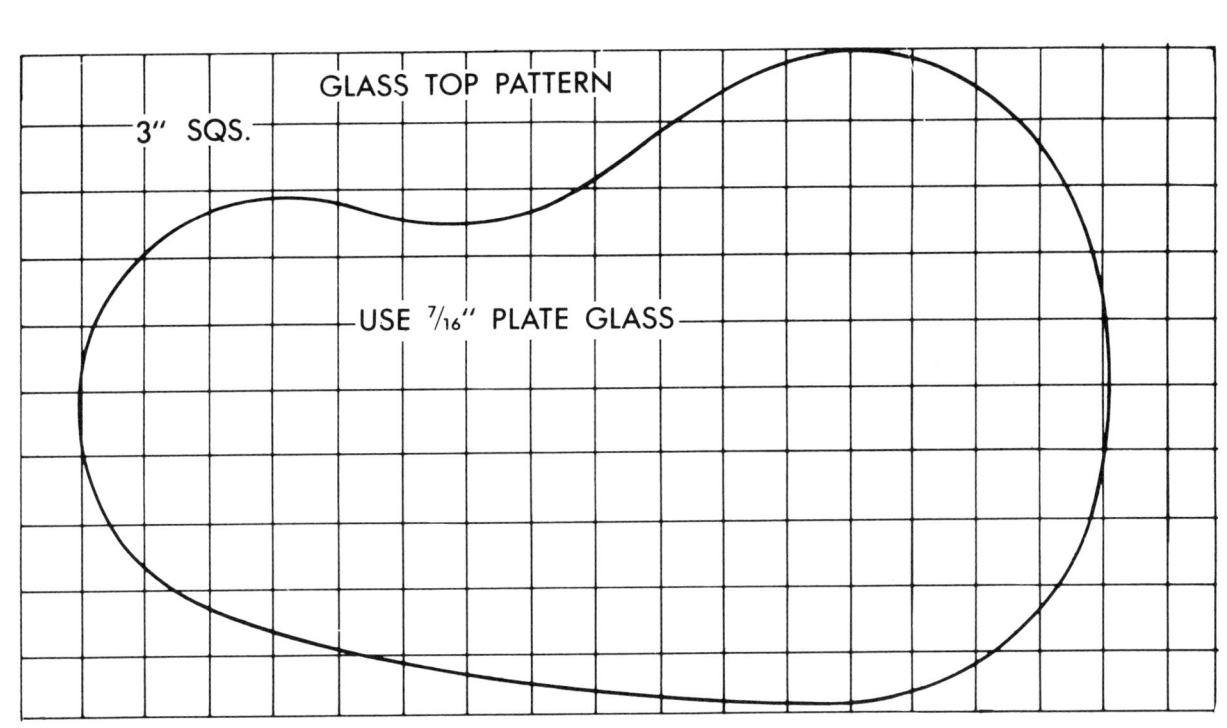
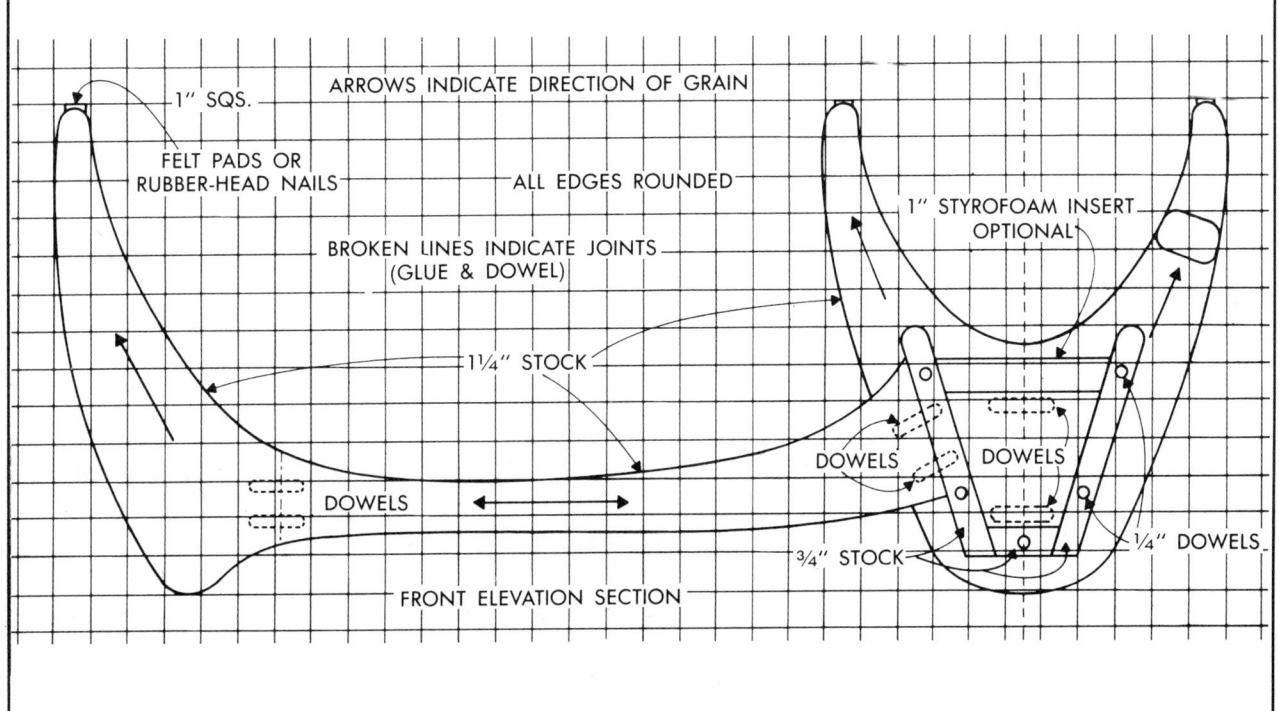

Wrought iron-base coffee table

Ornamental "wrought iron" combined with a glass top creates a truly distinctive coffee table, and no welding is required. All joints are assembled with blind rivets, which eliminates the need for a welder and the jigs and fixtures required to hold the sections while they are being welded.

The various shaped ornamental pieces are bent cold from mild steel. The jig used is made by drilling two holes in a block of steel to accept two steel rods, spaced slightly more than the thickness of the steel flats that are bent into curved shapes.

In use the jig is clamped in a vise and the work passed between the rods. The metal is bent slightly, moved a little, then bent again, to create a smooth, sweeping curve with no kinks. The 1/8 in. steel flats will not require heating, but can be bent cold. The heavier material, such as the rods used for the legs, may require being heated to a cherry red with a propane torch to permit bending them into the required "hairpin" shapes.

To assure uniformity and simplify construction, all pieces are cut to size before bending. Before cutting, however, make one test piece of each shape to determine the correct length. Bend the length to fit a pattern you have drawn full size. If your first section is too short, you can lengthen it; if too long, you can cut it and note the difference in length, so you can cut the other pieces to the right size.

You also can bend one section to shape and use it as a pattern for the other pieces. Because of the type construction, slight variations in shape will not be noticeable, and will lend a "hand-shaped" look to the finished table.

The upper and lower table frames are made from 1/2 in. angle, notched and bent as shown.

Steel flats are bent in jig made by inserting two rods in steel block, spaced apart to accept the metal as shown.

Angles for top and bottom of table frame are notched and bent. They should be positioned flat in vise, bent.

Scrolls were drilled first here; we suggest clamping the assembly, drilling through the angle and scroll at the same time to assure alignment of holes.

Triangular cherrywood coffee table

Blind rivets are used to assemble the scrolls to the angles, thus eliminating the need for welding and clamping.

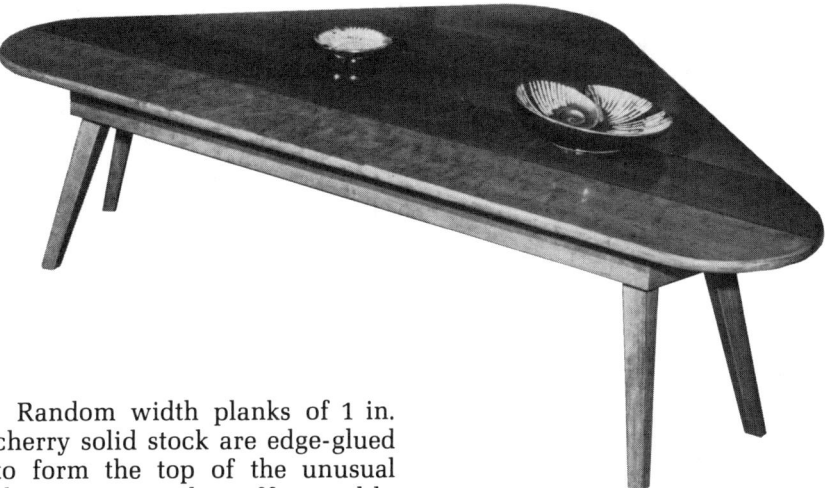

The joint is located on one of the long sides of the frame, and is joined by using a short length of steel flat, and four rivets.

Legs are bent from 5/16 or 3/8 in. diameter rod. Use a piece of rod longer than required and grip it at the center in the vise. Bend the other end around to create the hairpin shape, then cut off the excess.

The scrolls can be drilled first, then the locations of the holes marked on the angles, or the assembly can be clamped and holes drilled through the angles and scrolls at the same time. The latter method is more accurate in aligning the holes for the rivets.

When attaching the legs to the angle frames, longer rivets will be required. Note that the rivets may project slightly above the angle frame in which the glass sits. Peen these rivets down, or use strips of felt or rubber on the angle to support the glass above the rivets.

Wire-brush the metal and paint it flat white or, preferably, flat black.

MATERIALS LIST

Legs, 5/16" or 3/8" dia. steel rod x 37-1/4" (4)
Frame, 1/2" x 1/2" x 96" steel angle (2)
Brace, 1/8" x 1/2" x 2" (2)
Leg scroll, 1/8" x 1/2" x 15" (4)
Side scrolls, 1/8" x 1/2" x 15" (12)
End scrolls, 1/8" x 1/2" x 13-1/2" (8)
Rivets, medium length (50)
Rivets, long (24)
Glass, 1/4" x 17-7/8" x 30-7/8" (1)

Random width planks of 1 in. cherry solid stock are edge-glued to form the top of the unusual three-cornered coffee table shown. There are two legs at each of the three corners of the table.

Start construction by edge-gluing the trued lengths of stock to form a rectangle on which the triangular shape can be drawn. The planks are positioned parallel to the longer side of the table. Locate the center of what will be the long side of the table, then measure 43 in. from the center in both directions and make a mark. It may be necessary to temporarily position a scrap piece of stock at the ends of the glued-up top to permit marking the 43 in. distance. Now, from the center of the edge, draw a line at right angles, and at least 45 in. long. From this 45 in. mark draw a line to each of the points on the long edge of the top that are 43 in. from the center of the edge. The result will be a triangle with two legs of equal length, the third leg being longer.

Measure up 27 in. from the long edge and make a mark. From this point draw an arc with a compass or trammel points, having a radius of 12 in. The positions of the centers for drawing the 6 in. radius at each of the other corners can be found in different ways. For example, if the triangle is not cut to shape, bisect each of the angles with a compass or trammel points, as in Figs. 1 through 3, and in Fig. 5. You will note in Figs. 1 through 3 that it was necessary to temporarily fit a scrap of stock at the end of the glued-up top to permit drawing the complete triangle. Using the point of the triangle as a center, two arcs with equal radii are drawn to intersect the sides of the triangle. From the latter two points two more equal-length arcs are drawn so they intersect inside the triangle. To bisect the angle, draw a line from the intersection of the last two arcs to the point of the triangle. Now, adjust your square to a 6 in. length and move it along the edge of the tabletop until it just touches the bisecting line. Make a mark at this point and use it as the center for drawing an arc with a 6 in. radius. The operation is repeated at the opposite corner.

An alternate method of finding the centers for drawing the 6 in. arcs, if the tabletop is cut to triangular shape, is simply to set your square at 6 in. and move it along the adjacent edges of the table, drawing a line as you move the square. The intersection of the two lines will be the center for the 6 in. arc. Both methods are in Fig. 5.

To determine the various angles between the pieces of the apron, draw lines 3/4 in. apart as indicated to show the positions of

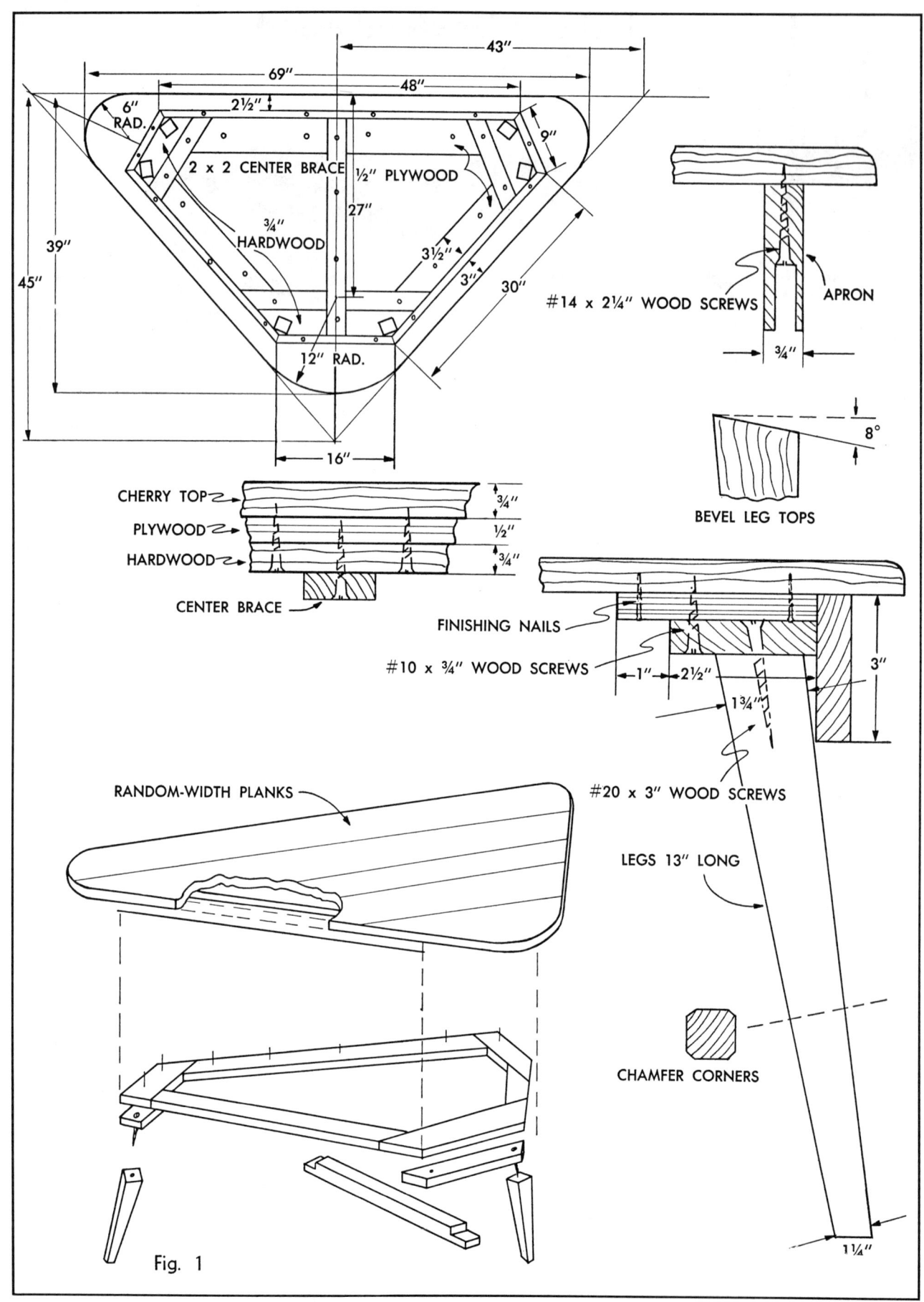
Fig. 1

the apron members. At the various intersections, draw lines to make the angles. Pick up the angles with the aid of a sliding T-bevel as shown in Fig. 5, then transfer them to your saw and cut the angles on the apron pieces. Attach the apron to the tabletop with screws driven up through holes that are counterbored in the apron, Fig. 4.

The pairs of beveled legs are cut at top and bottom to provide the correct angle, then are attached to hardwood pieces with screws. The hardwood members then are attached to the strips of 1/2 in. plywood that are attached to the underside of the top with glue, wood screws and finishing nails. Be sure that the fasteners are short enough so that none penetrate the top. Finally, attach the center brace.

Round the edges of the top, then sand the top with progressively finer grits until a smooth finish is obtained. Dust thoroughly, then apply a paste filler, thinned as per the manufacturer's instructions. When it has set, sand again, then apply your favorite finish — clear shellac, lacquer or paste wax.

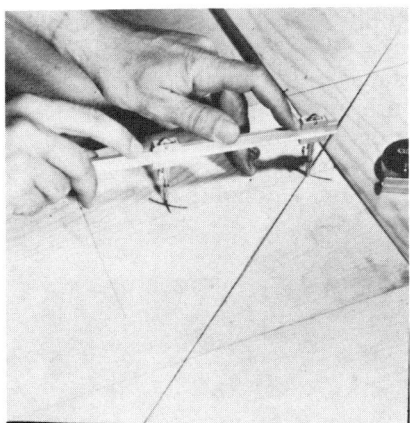

After top boards are assembled, use scrap to extend triangle, bisect angle.

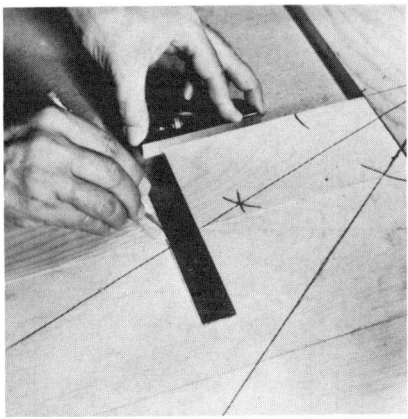

Slide square along edge until 6 in. mark intersects line that bisects angle.

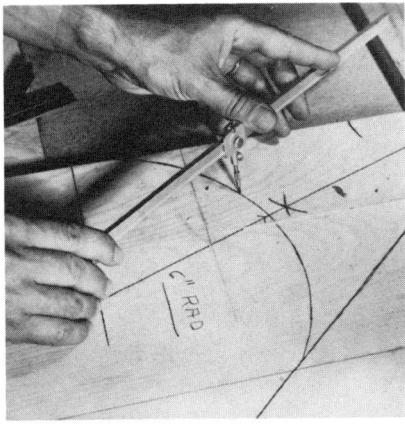

At intersection of 6 in. line and line bisecting angle, set compass, make arc.

Apron is attached to underside of tabletop by screws driven up through apron in counterbored holes.

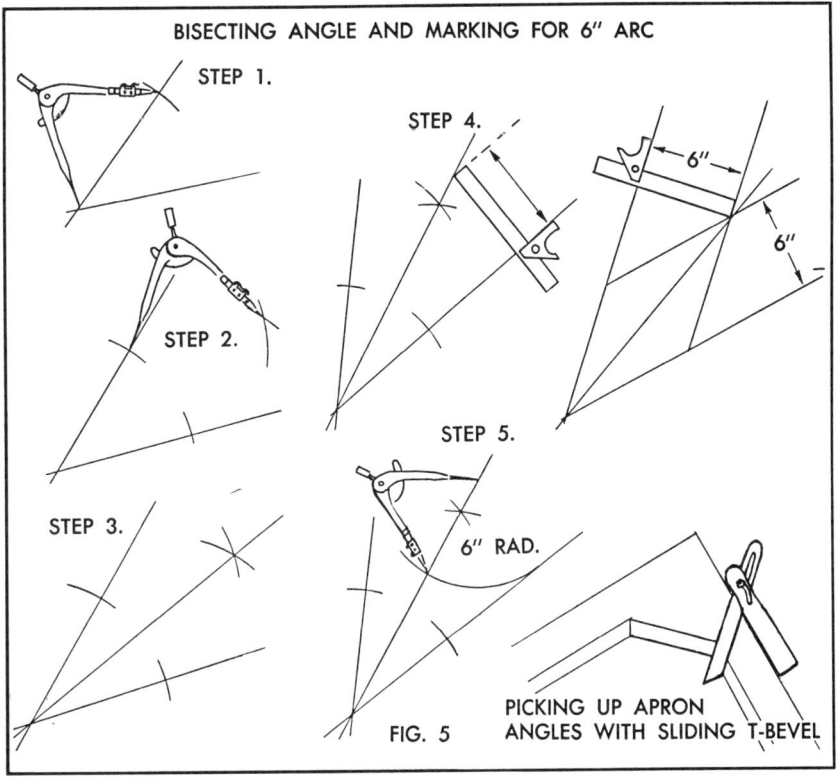

FIG. 5

English butler-tray serving table

An authentic antique English butler-tray table in mahogany or walnut is an expensive and rare item today. However, you can make this reproduction rather easily, using common hand tools to work plywood and pine.

For experienced craftsmen, the basic design invites embellishment—perhaps marquetry and molded edges for the tray, carved solid hardwood legs and rails for the table frame.

Begin work by marking out the oval-shaped tray on a 3/4 in. plywood rectangle. Carefully mark the inner leaf edges as shown. Note the position of the upright leaves in the photograph, and the relationship of the corners. Mark handhold positions on the leaves.

Mark for hinges and chisel out mortises. The hinges used should be designed for this special application. If you can't get butler-tray hinges locally, they are available from mail-order woodworking supply houses.

Drill and saw the handholds as marked. Finish shaping the holes with a rasp, smooth with sandpaper, then slightly bevel the edges to avoid splintering.

Carefully cut along the lines to separate the end leaves from the tray bottom, then cut off the longer leaves. Cut the arcs on the leaves and temporarily reassemble the pieces to make sure they form a perfect oval. You can cut out the entire oval before separating the leaves from the bottom, but this will deprive you of useful straight edges that help guide the other cuts.

Glue and nail together the leg components as shown. The rails should be glued and doweled to the legs. Internal corner-block reinforcements are optional for extra strength if desired.

Align the tray bottom on the frame rails and temporarily clamp it in place. Mark the underside of the tray bottom for cleats along the front and back. The cleats will permit the frame to hold the tray securely, yet allow its easy removal when required.

Unclamp the tray bottom, cut 3/4 in. square stock cleats to fit and drill pilot holes for three equally-spaced screws in each cleat. Hinge the leaves in place, then invert the tray and attach the cleats to the tray bottom with glue and screws.

Apply veneer tape to the edges of the tray. Thoroughly sand all surfaces and wipe with a tack rag before finishing. Use a good penetrating sealer to protect the wood. Any finish you use should be water- and alcohol-resistant.

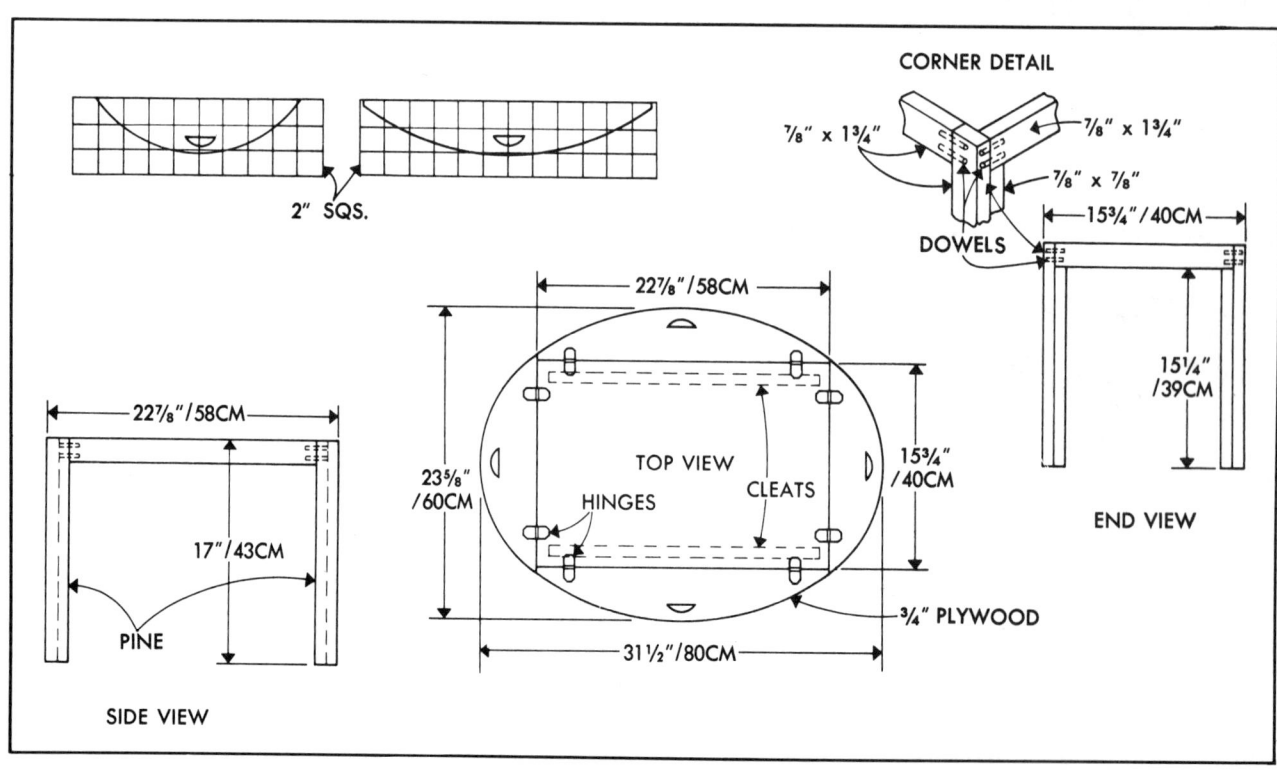

Basic tea cart

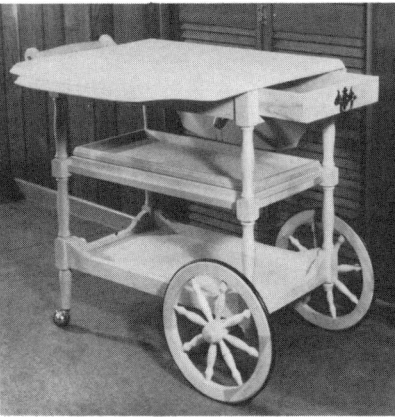

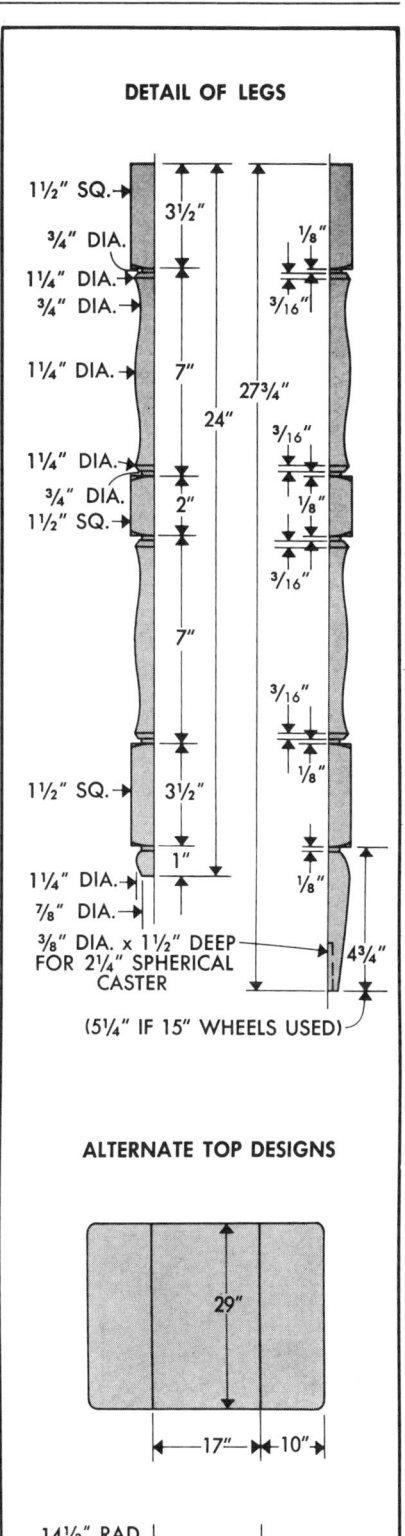

Almost any kind of close-grained hardwood can be used to make this practical tea cart. The original shown was made from maple, then given a "cinnamon" stain.

Also note that while this tea cart has 14 in. wooden wheels, 15 in. plastic wheels can be used by adding 1/2 in. to the turned portion at the bottom of the caster legs. Wheels must be purchased.

Start assembly by edge-gluing strips of stock for the top and leaves. Alternate strips are inverted to keep heartwood and sapwood faces opposed to minimize warping. Hardwood plywood also could be used, with flat edges covered with veneer tape.

The solid top and leaves perhaps could be surface planed at a local lumberyard that has a 24 in. planer. Patience and a belt sander also can be used.

The four legs are turned as indicated and drilled for dowel joints, except for the 45 degree notch in which the center shelf is glued.

After cutting all pieces to size and sanding them, construction is started by making the end assemblies. Watch the size and positioning of the short upper stretchers; on the drawer end this is 1/2 in. thick and is fitted below the drawer. On the handle end the stretcher is 3/4 in. stock and it is positioned flush with the tops of the caster legs. Glue and clamp these two assemblies square, wiping off any excess glue.

When the glue has set on the end assemblies, "dry-assemble" the various rails and stretchers between the ends to make sure everything fits properly. You may need to sand the center shelf slightly at the corners so it fits easily into the notches in the legs.

Disassemble the parts, apply glue and reassemble, clamping firmly and checking to make sure everything is square, and that all four legs are vertical. It would be a good idea at this point to trial-fit the wheels and casters to make sure they all contact the floor evenly.

Wheels come with a suitable axle, while the casters require boring holes in the legs to accept sleeves into which the caster shanks fit.

The handy tray that stores on the center shelf fits on two rails, and has felt pads on the underside to prevent marring the wood.

The top and leaves now are hinged together. Place them upside down on a blanket or other protective surface for this job. Notch the upper edges of the top side rails to provide clearance for the hinges, which are screwed to the underside of the top and leaves and not recessed.

The assembled tea cart now is inverted onto the top and attached by screws driven through counterbored holes in the top rails.

You may wish to fit the drawer in place before attaching the top, but the handle is screwed on last, and positioned to suit the user; either slightly up or down from the position shown, as required.

Attach the drop-leaf supports, then check their action when the cart is set on its wheels and casters. The cart is now ready for finishing.

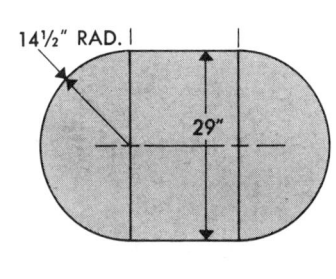

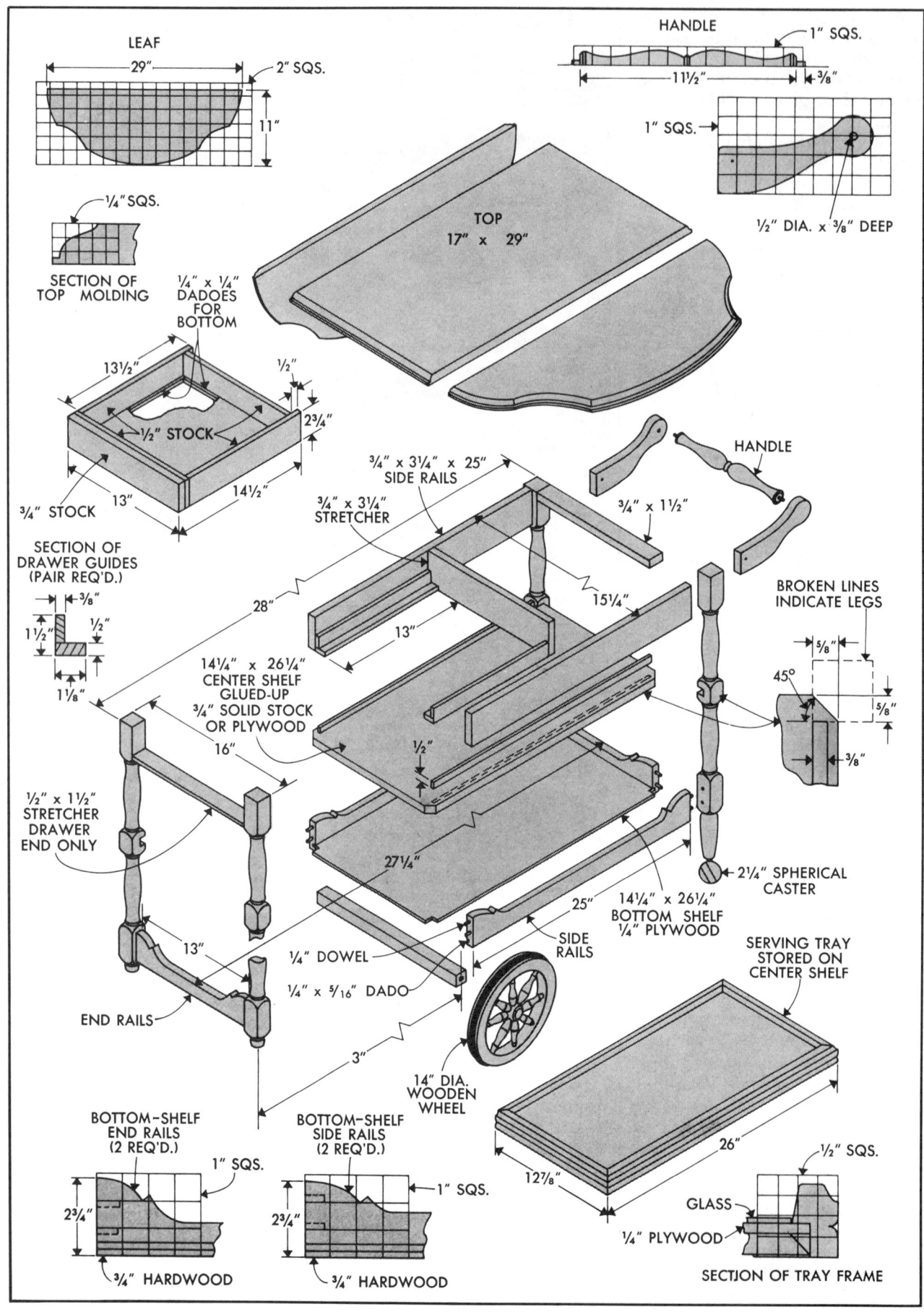

Colonial style serving cart

Attractive and functional, this trim serving cart with its authentic Colonial styling is a nice addition to the living room, besides being useful on the patio or near the pool area. Buckets on each end will hold magazines or sewing needs, or if lined with aluminum or copper, they could hold ice or even plants. The 14 in. rubber-tired tea cart wheels make the cart easy to move around.

Made from hardwoods selected to complement your decor, the cart can be constructed with hand or power tools. The only problem might involve turning the back legs, handle and the buckets. The legs and handle can be purchased, and the buckets can be left rough or sanded smooth with a power sander.

Start with the buckets first, by cutting the required angle of 11-1/4

Cut bucket staves, dado them and assemble with 1/8 in. splines and lots of glue. Clamp tightly with rope.

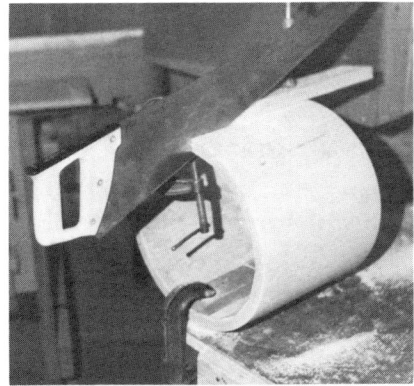

After bucket is turned smooth, cut it in half along opposing joints using a fine-toothed saw and guide strip.

degrees on the 16 staves. It might be a good idea to practice a bit here, as just a slight error in angle can result in one or more of the joints being open. Make the staves a little longer than 10 in. as they can be trimmed on the lathe. You might also make a couple of extra staves in case one or two do not fit properly. Cut dadoes along the length of the staves to hold the 1/8 in. splines.

Carefully assemble all the staves into a circle and check for misalignment. Then use lots of glue and assemble the bucket as shown in the photo and clamp, using a strong rope and the "tourniquet" method.

The bucket can be turned on a lathe using a jig as shown in the photograph. To make the jig, cut two pieces of stock 2 in. wide and 2 in. shorter than the staves and screw them to the inside of the bucket on opposing staves. Attach two other pieces to the ends of these strips and mark the center of each. Attach to the faceplate and the tailstock of the lathe and you are in business. If you don't have a lathe, sand the bucket round or leave it rough.

After turning, cut the bucket in half along opposing joints, using a piece of scrap stock as a guide for a fine-toothed saw. Sand the rough edges smooth for a tight fit against the ends of the cart.

The legs and handle are simple turnings, or they can be purchased items cut to the correct length with a similar shape filed in them.

Cut the bottom and ends of the cart to the proper shape, using the squared drawings. Assemble them with glue and #10 x 2 in. FH wood screws through the bottom. The shelf is secured to the sides by glue and two #6 x 1-1/2 in. FH screws. The screws are concealed under the hinges on the lids.

Attach the buckets to the bottom and sides with #10 x 1-1/2 in. FH screws, driving the screws through the sides and up through the bottom. The screws in the sides can be concealed with plugs, or left exposed. If exposed, use chrome-plated roundhead screws and finishing washers.

Drill 3/8 in. holes in one end of the two back legs to take the caster sleeves. Then press the legs into holes bored in the bottom brace. Drill holes at a 5 degree angle.

The axle support is attached to the bottom with glue and held firmly by two quarter-round brackets.

The bucket lids are fitted in place with 1-1/2 in. butt hinges, mortised into the edges.

Using a coping or a band saw, cut the scalloped shelf edges and the handle arms from 1/2 in. stock. Glue the former in place. The handle arms are attached to the outer edge of the sides using glue and 1-1/2 in. RH chrome screws and finishing washers. First, press the turned handle into the 1/2 in. holes and glue and screw them. They can be held in place with tiny brads from underneath, but the screws and finishing washers will give a uniform appearance to the cart.

You can make your own axle assembly or purchase one. If you do purchase one, it must have several inches cut from the middle, as factory-built assemblies are too long.

Now give all parts a good sanding and apply the finish of your choice. Then add the metal banding to the buckets, the back casters and the rubber-tired wheels.

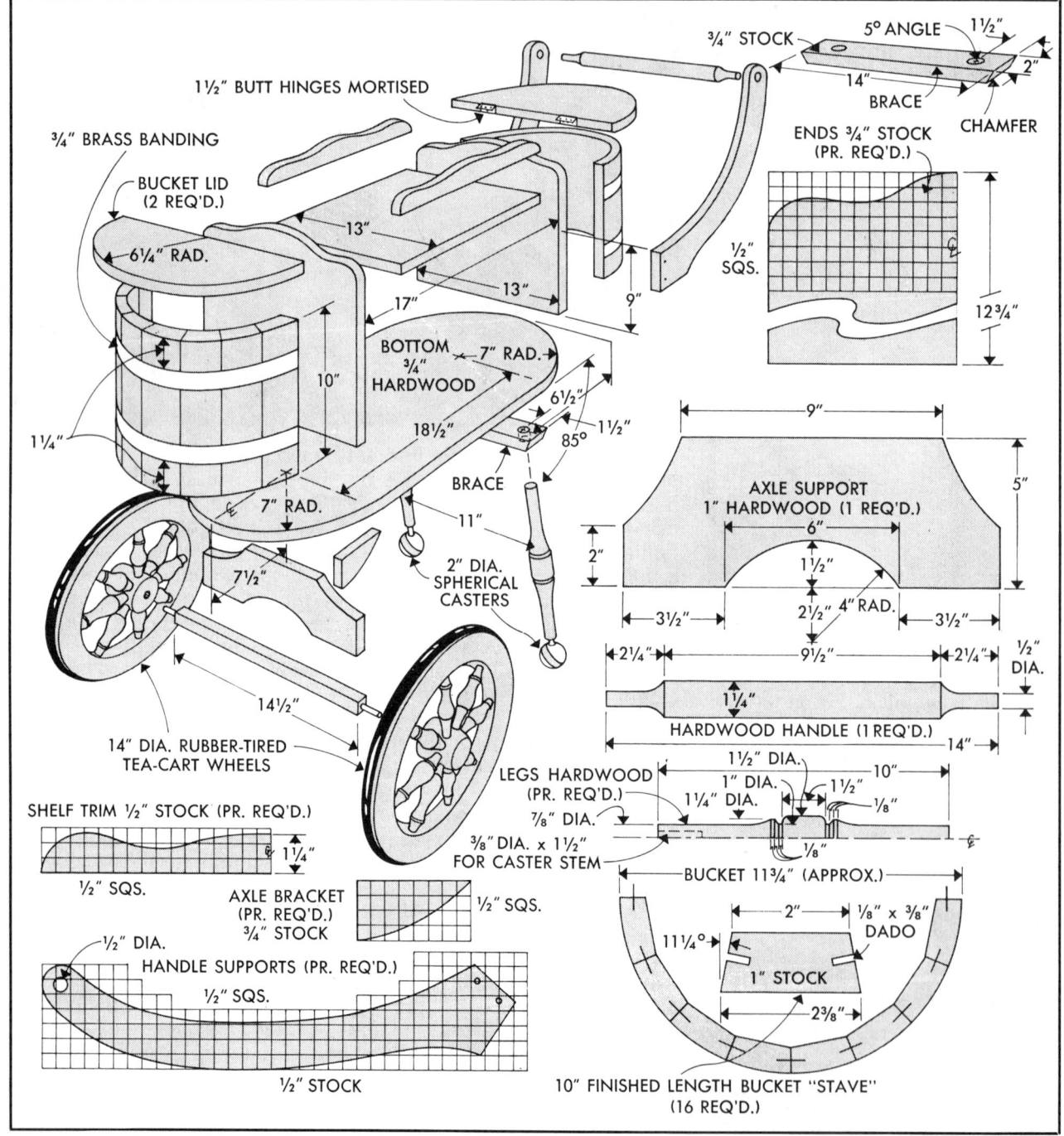

Contemporary Danish tea cart

Danish-inspired is the design of this contemporary tea cart that is versatile enough to double as a refreshment wagon on the patio.

Solid walnut was used on the original for the side supports and the shelf frames. Any good cabinet-grade hardwood can be substituted. Choose a wood to match other contemporary furniture you may have. Wood-grained plastic laminate was applied as covering for the shelves cut from 1/4 in. tempered hardboard. While a plastic insert made by melting crystals was added to the top of the cart shown, you may wish to use laminate instead. Or, ceramic tile could be used to create an attractive accent.

Start construction by cutting and mitering the shelf frames. Note that the lower frame is 1-1/2 in. high, the middle and top shelf are 1 in. high. Dadoes are cut on the inside of all four members of the two lower shelves, but none is cut in one end member of the top shelf. This is the end that forms a handle. The top shelf requires two dividers. Dadoes are cut on two sides of one divider, only on one side of the other.

Cut the hardboard to size for the three shelves, and glue on the laminate, using contact adhesive. All dadoes are 3/8 in. deep, and are cut wide enough for a "slip-fit" of the hardboard-laminate assembly. Assemble the two lower shelves with glue, driving a wood screw through the ends of each side member, in a counterbored hole that can later be plugged.

Plastic insert for top shelf is made by melting crystals in oven. Insert is made oversize, cut down to fit the frame.

Screws are driven through the shelf members into the side supports, thus are hidden. Also use glue in joints.

The plastic insert on the top of the model shown is made from crystals that can be obtained at hobby shops. The crystals are poured into a container to a thickness about equal to the hardboard-laminate shelves, then baked in an oven at about 350° so they melt and flow to form the panel. Make it slightly oversize, then cut it to fit in the dadoes cut in the shelf frame and the divider. You now assemble the top shelf, using glue and screws through the side members into the ends. Again, use counterbored holes and plug them.

Make a pattern for the side supports, enlarging the squared drawing. Each side support is made in three pieces, being joined with half-laps at the upper corners. The three shelves are attached to the side supports by driving screws through from the inside of the shelf frames into the supports.

Blocks cut from 1 in. stock are glued to the corners of the underside of the lower shelf and spherical casters are screwed to the blocks. Cut the blocks about 4 in. square. Position the casters so they are flush with the end and side when swiveled to the end and side.

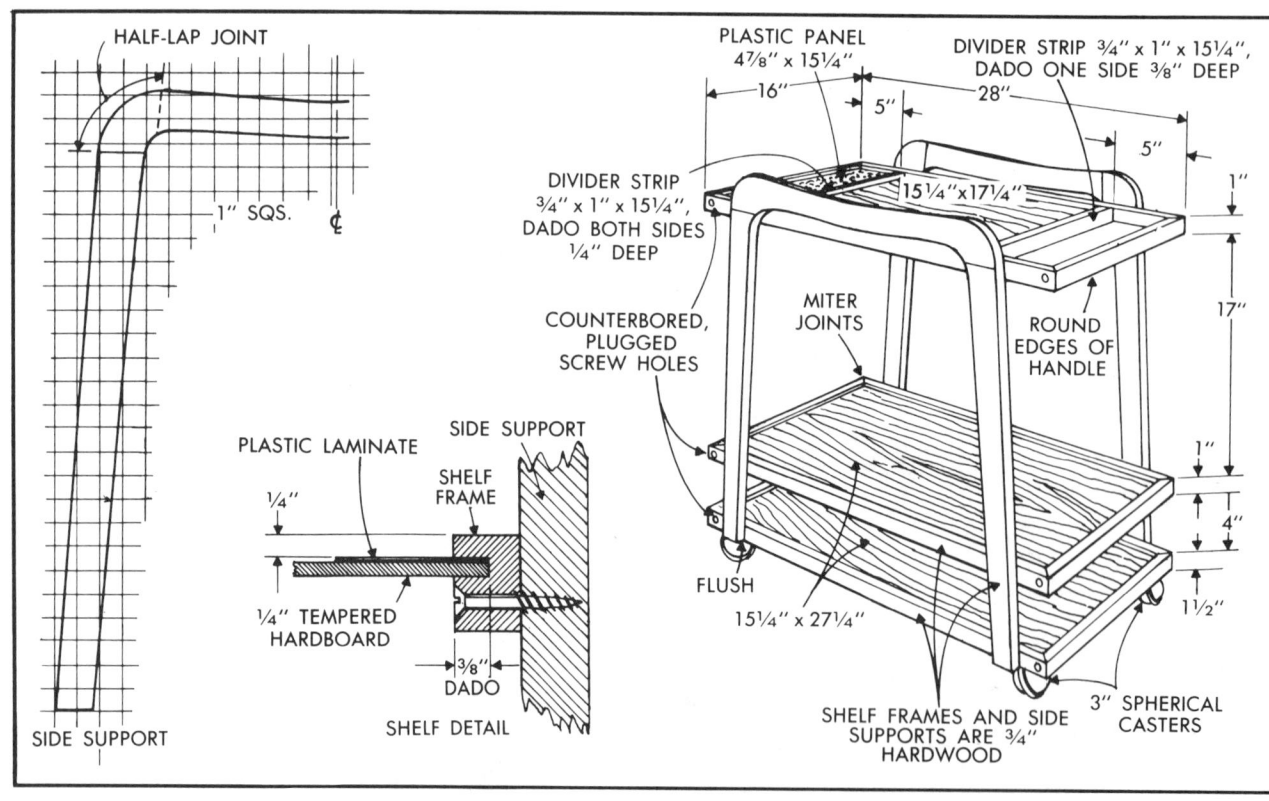

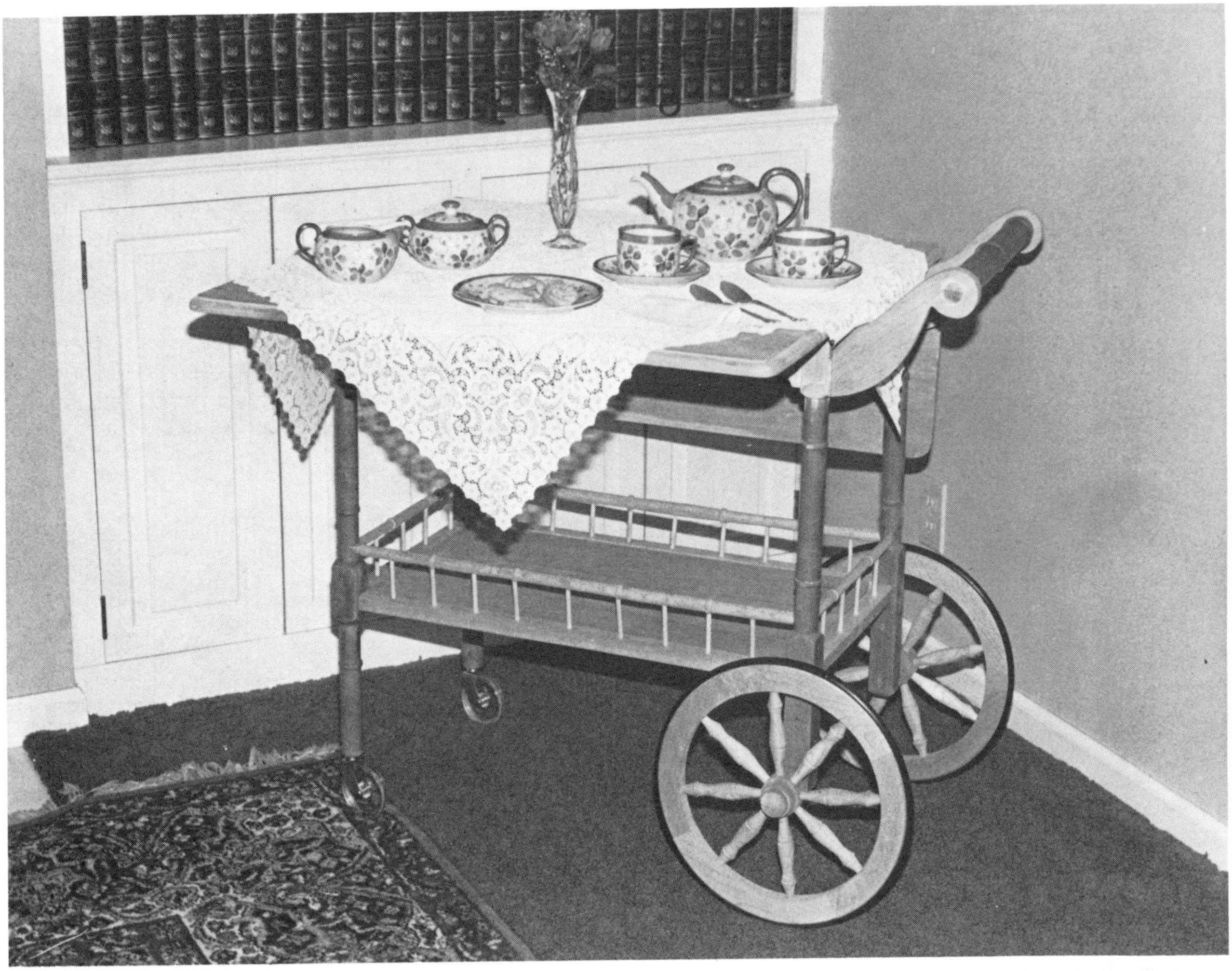

Chippendale-Chinese style tea cart

This version of the traditional tea cart is in the style of Chippendale when he worked with oriental motifs in his furniture.

If not available locally, wheels and appropriate spindle casters can be ordered from mail-order woodworking supply companies. Because tea cart wheels present a challenge of the first magnitude for even the most accomplished home craftsman, it is recommended wheels be purchased, so no details are provided for making them.

The first step in construction is to turn the four legs. Each pair has the same profile, but the pair in which the wheels are fitted has a longer square portion at the bottom. Obtain the wheels and casters before you bore the holes for mounting the wheels. The casters are installed in the ends of the longer legs, then the cart frame, without the top and leaves, leveled. The wheels, with stub axles, then are placed alongside the shorter legs and the holes for the axles marked.

When you receive the ready-made wheels, they may well include a wooden axle with two steel axle stubs in the ends. The axle stubs may be grooved, and the wheels fitted with a metal sleeve much like that used for spindle casters. The wheels then simply "snap" onto the axles.

For this tea cart, the wooden portion of the axle is split and the metal stubs removed. The stub axles then are fitted into the wheels, and the stub axles slipped into the drilled holes in the two shorter legs. The projecting portion of each axle is marked with a

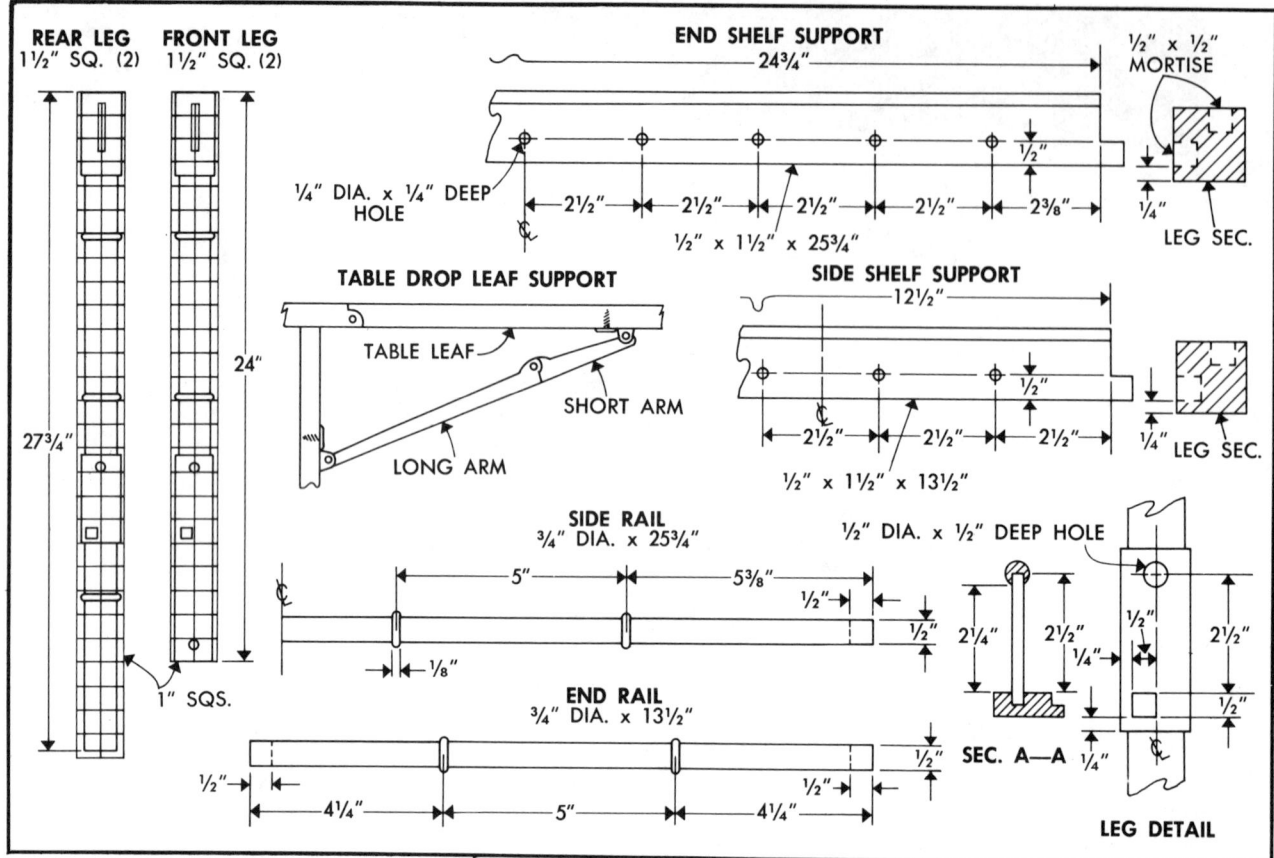

hacksaw and the axles removed. The stubs are cut with a hacksaw to be about 1/8 in. shorter than the mark made on them when they were in place. This allows inserting a wooden plug to cover the ends of the stub axles on the inside surfaces of the legs.

The axles are kept in place by drilling through the legs and axles with a 1/8 in. bit and tapping in a slender finishing nail.

If you choose cherry wood for building this tea cart you may find it to be a bit splintery when the "bamboo joints" are turned on the legs and various spindles, so allow a bit of extra stock and be sure your lathe chisels are sharp when making the turnings.

The turning for the handle is thick enough in diameter, and short enough, so that it presents no real problems in turning. The 3/4 in. tenons on the ends were made a bit long, then were sawed to precise fit length when the handle was assembled.

When you make the spindles that are used for the railing around the shelf you may very well have a problem with the slender turnings, and a steady-rest may be required. A shop-made steady-rest of wood, with a V-notch in a vertical piece of wood, serves quite well.

Some of the turnings were stained and finished while still in the lathe; however, the slender turnings were not, as it is difficult to keep the finishing materials off the ends of the spindles where they are to be glued into the legs.

Mortising can be done on a drill press with the help of a mortising bit or hand fashioned with a wood chisel. One place that might take some cutting and fitting is where the L-shape shelf supports enter the lower portions of the legs. It might be necessary to angle the ends of the tenons on the L-shape pieces slightly, as they may possibly contact each other where mortises intersect. Whether or not this trimming will be necessary depends on how much of the original 1-1/2 in. square of the leg remains when the final assembly is made.

To aid assembly further, place the L-shaped pieces and their matching spindles side by side and locate the holes for the 1/4 in. spindles with the aid of a square. For another tip, keep the square portions of the ends of the turnings on until after you have bored the holes for the spindles. This will prevent them from turning while being drilled.

One might be tempted to allow the mortises at the tops of the legs to open all the way to the top. This risk is that this weakens the top joints and all one's hard work may be ruined by splitting out the thin walls when the part is put into service.

Should you be working with uninterestingly grained wood, want to hide puttied mistakes, or for some other reason want to depart from the usual stain and varnish finish, you might consider alternatives — a Chinese black, red and gold lacquer approach, a solid bright blue, green, red or orange antiqued finish, or some other finish that will fit well in the setting in which the finished cart will be used.

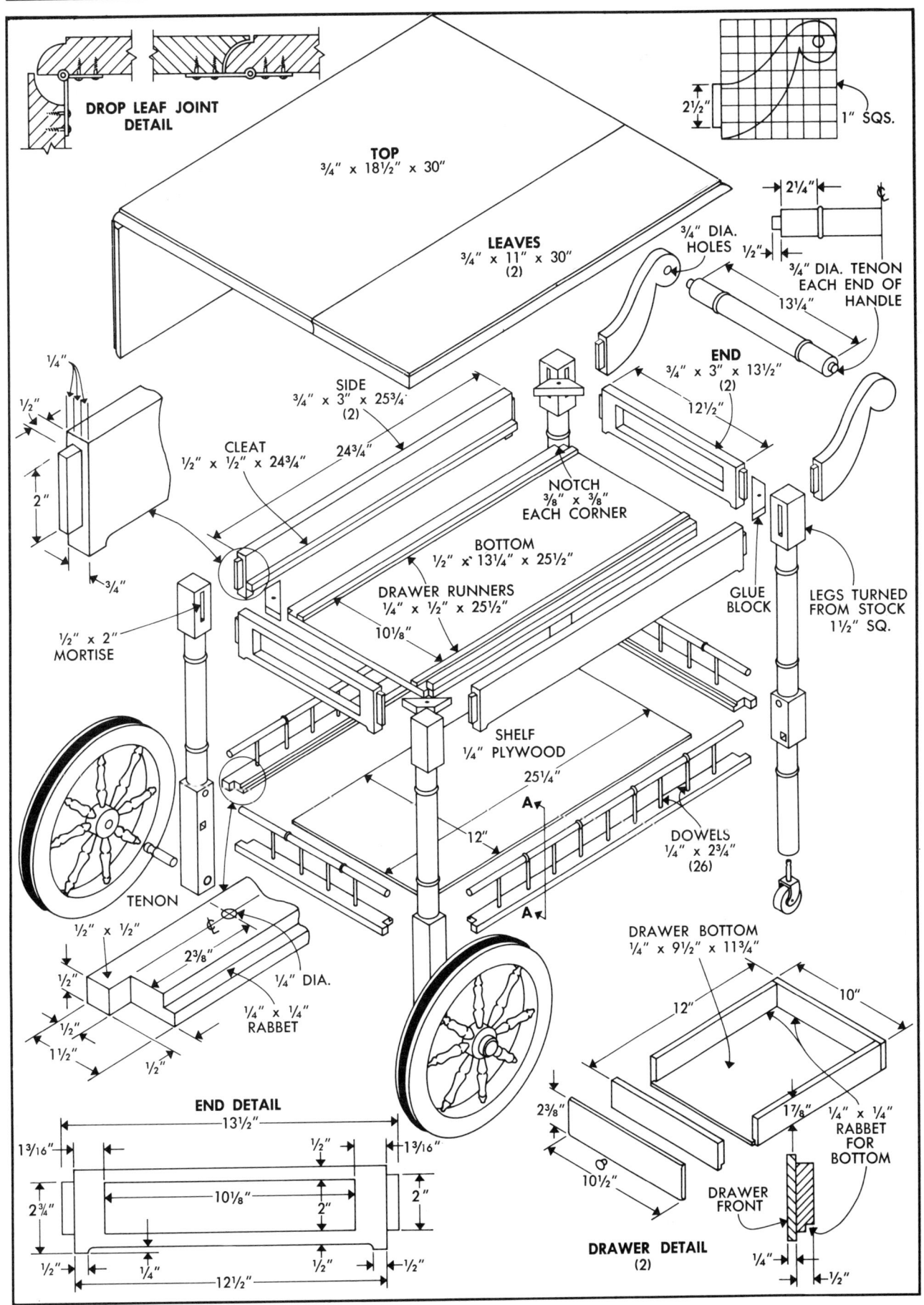

Colonial tea table with cabriole legs

This classically simple tea table from the second quarter of the eighteenth century was a gift of Mrs. Gustav Radeke to the Museum of Art, Rhode Island School of Design, Providence. We are indebted to the school for permission to publish the photograph and to measure and draw the table.

The graceful cabriole legs project upward to form the corner posts of the table, terminate at the bottom in pointed, Dutch feet. The legs give the table its charm, and also present a challenge to the craftsman.

The rectangular top is supported in the rabbeted apron. The curved molding on the top can be made with a shaper, router or molding cutter in a table or radial arm saw. Although the apron is indicated as being in one piece, it may be necessary to make the lower molding as an extra member and glue it on. It is difficult and expensive to get hardwood thick enough to make the apron in one piece. You also might want to use hardwood-faced plywood for both top and apron. The lower molding then would have to be a separate piece. Also, change the dimensions of the rabbet, which is shown for a top 1-1/8 in. thick to be set in an apron 7/8 in. thick.

Quite likely it might be necessary to glue up a number of pieces of stock to make a block for each leg. Stock 3 in. square is available from various wood supply houses, however. On the original table the legs and corner posts of the table are a single piece. It may be easier for some craftsmen to make the legs and posts separately and dowel them together.

If this tea table is your first project with cabriole legs we suggest you practice cutting the legs from softwood before tackling the more expensive hardwood. Cut just to the line, then finish shaping the legs with file and sandpaper. For complete details on how to make cabriole legs, read about the Queen Anne table that follows.

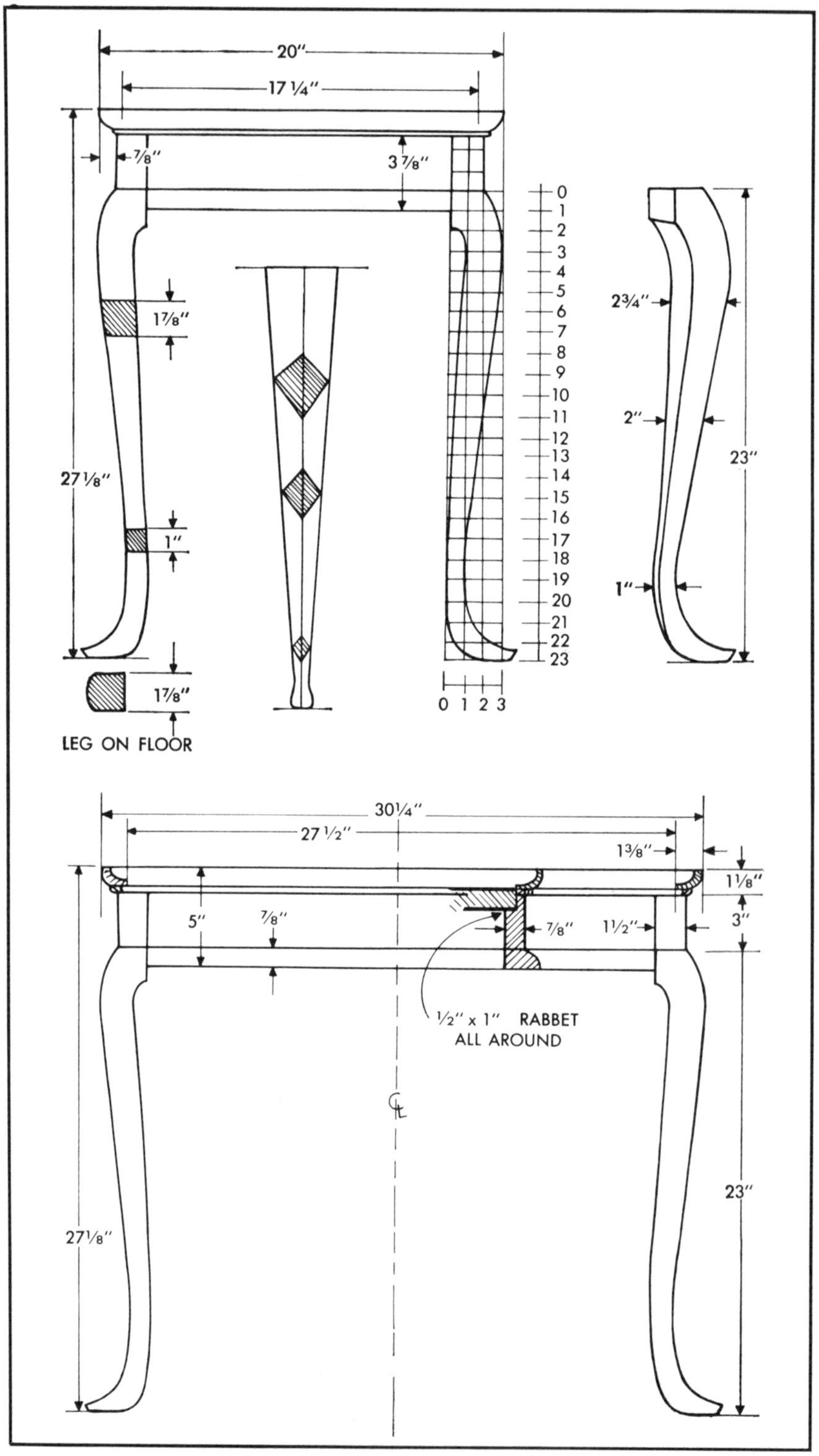

Elegant Queen Ann table

Modeled after the fine pieces made in eighteenth-century England, this Queen Anne tea table can be assembled with a simplified, modern technique using ready-made Queen Anne cabriole legs. For the craftsman who would rather make his own, we show a pattern in a squared drawing. The pattern can be modified, of course, by the more experienced craftsman who enjoys creating an individual design.

No matter how you change the design of the leg, remember the axiom that a vertical centerline through the top of the leg should intersect the center of the foot. Farther on are complete details on making cabriole legs.

Cut the four aprons to size and shape, miter the ends then glue and clamp them together on a flat surface. Be sure to let the glue set completely, as it will be the only thing holding the corners together until they are reinforced with the legs.

Unless you use ready-made legs that attach with plates, cut the legs as indicated and glue and screw them inside each corner of the apron assembly as shown. Reinforce them with the glue blocks as indicated.

Make the two frames, one of picture frame molding (purchased or made as detailed) and one of 1/2 in. stock. Glass is fitted in the rabbet of the molding—this should be plate glass at least 1/4 in. thick—then the molding is screwed to the frame of 1/2 in. stock.

If the top is to be tilted so you can use it for display or easy reading, install two hinges inside one long apron and on the long side of the frame assembly as indicated. Also install the prop and notched bracket. Position the prop to hold the top at any angle you wish.

If the optional candle trays are installed, replace the glass with a piece of 1/4 in. hardwood paneling so the "mechanism" is hidden.

Stain and finish to suit your decor. Apply a number of coats of varnish or lacquer for a deep, rich finish.

Now, for the details on how to make your own cabriole legs. Classic furniture for hundreds of years has been graced with the lovely curves of cabriole legs. As a point of information, the first such legs are thought to have been designed and created by a Chinese craftsman many centuries ago. The cabriole shape is based on the cyma curve; this is rather common in furniture decoration and consists of two reversed curves joined together. In the cabriole leg you see the upper portion of the leg with the outward

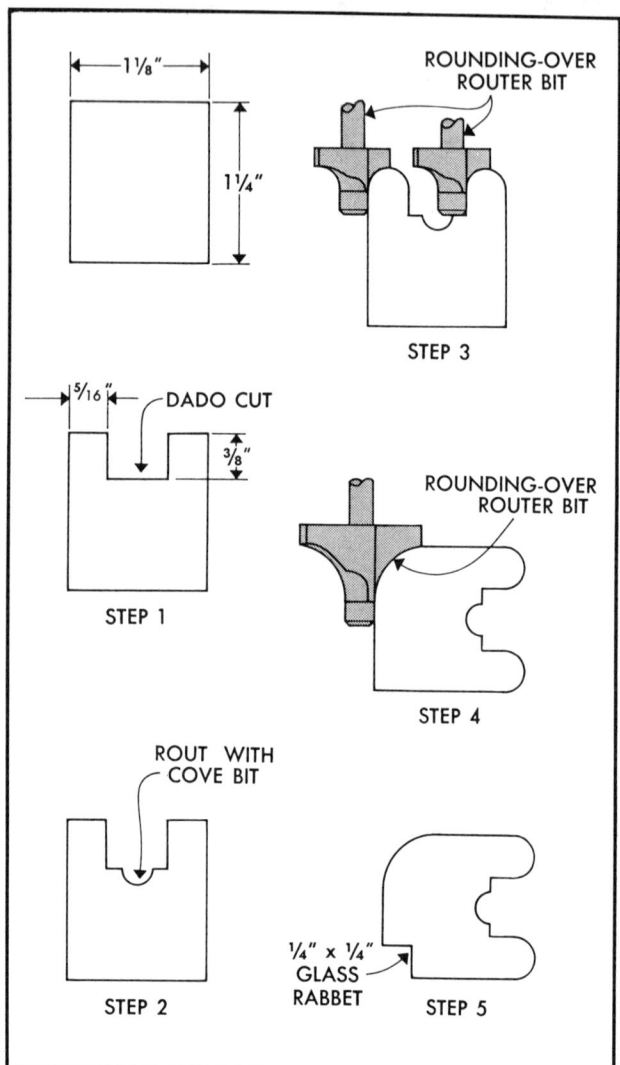

As an added feature, top tilts up to afford convenient reading position.

Profiles on lower edges of aprons are cut with portable jig saw, pieces saved. Jig saw or band saw can be used instead.

curve, the lower portion with the reversed inward curve.

Despite the simple design on which it is based, the cabriole leg exists in an almost infinite number of sizes and proportions. Early Georgian styling called for slightly heavier legs with a ball-and-claw foot. Many Louis XV pieces of furniture had a hoof-like foot that is now generally called the Queen Anne style. Provincial period furniture often had a more

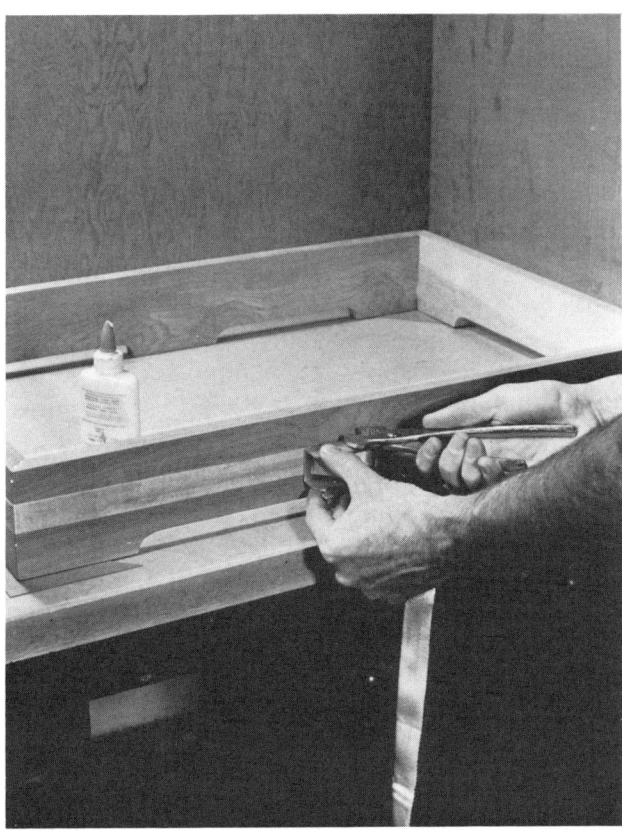
Ends of aprons are mitered, glue applied, then assembled and held with strap clamp. Check for square corners.

Holes for 1/4 or 5/16 in. dowels are drilled in lower edges of aprons. Thumb tack makes dowel-center tool to mark holes.

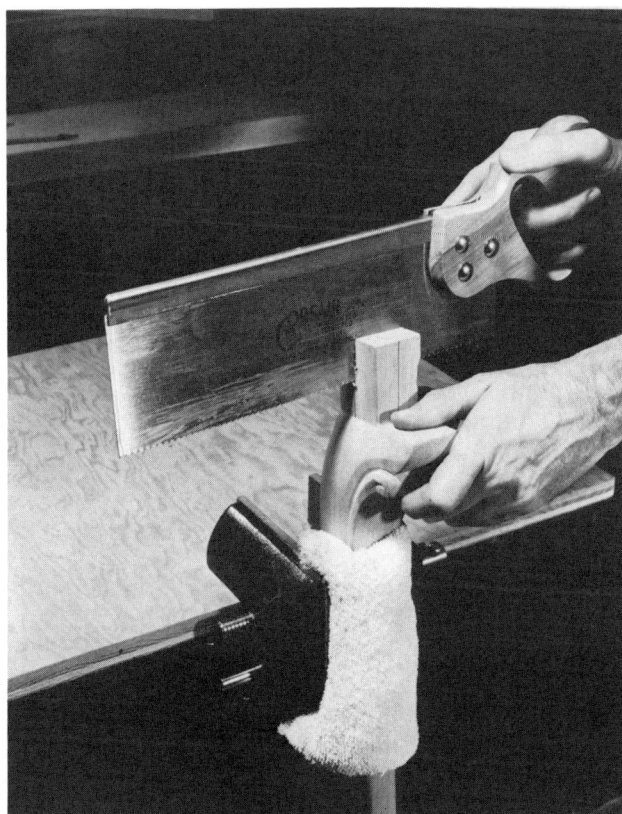
If ready-made legs are used, tops are cut to provide "shelf" 3/4 in. wide on which adjacent aprons rest.

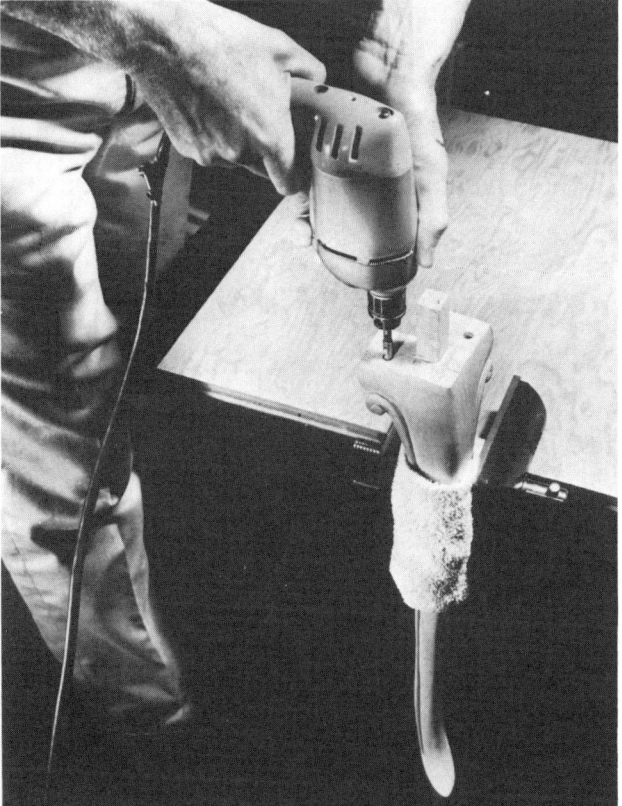
Matching holes are drilled in leg tops, with legs held in vise. Legs are padded to prevent vise damaging them.

Place dowels in legs, check fit to aprons. Make any necessary adjustments to assure perfect fit between legs and aprons.

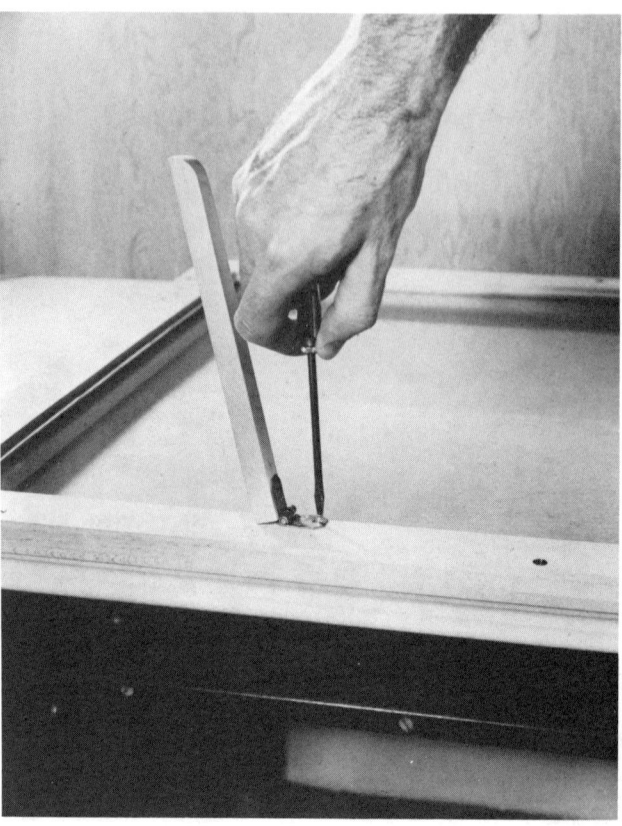

If you wish top to tilt up for display or for convenient reading or study, attach brace with 3/4 in. brass butt hinge.

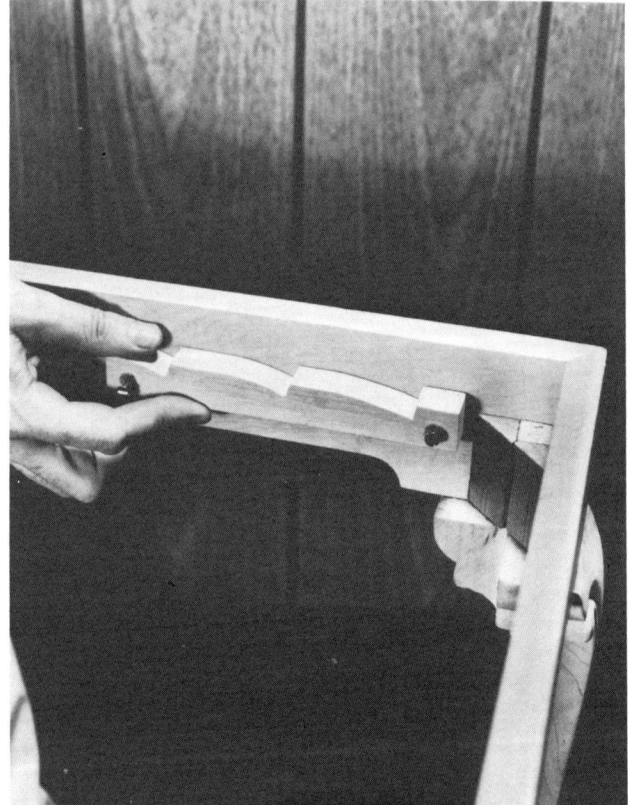

Notched hardwood bracket is screwed to inside of one or both side aprons to accept end of brace that holds up top.

Pressed-wood ornament is located at center of each long apron 1/4 in. above lower edge. Use glue and small brads.

Optional leg is ready-made type that fastens by means of metal plate. In this case, glue and screw triangular pieces.

Three of the screws that hold metal leg plate are driven into lower edges of adjacent aprons. Predrill holes.

Optional leg attached with metal plate is attractive and functional; not quite as graceful as leg used on original.

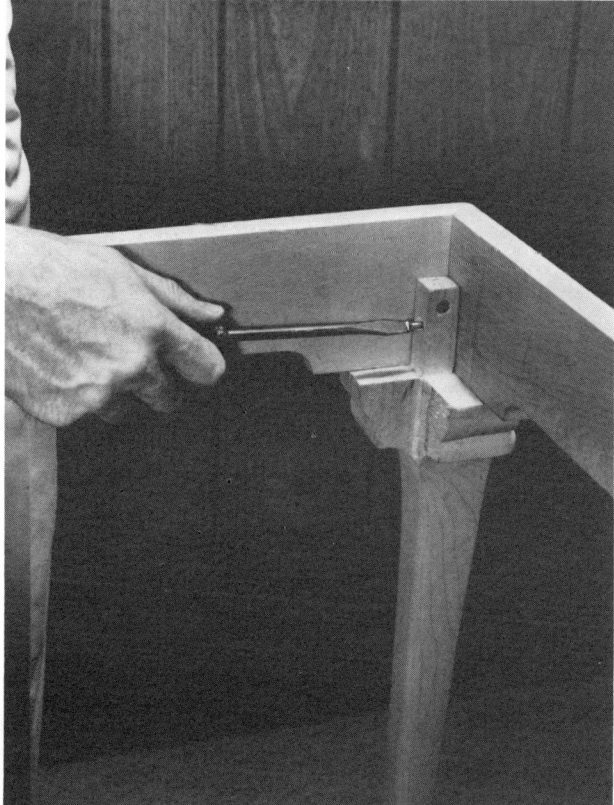

Projections on leg tops are cross-drilled for No. 8 x 1 in. brass screws. Glue is applied, screws driven into aprons.

Triangular blocks are glued to each side of each leg top to reinforce the attachment to the apron.

Picture-frame molding (made or purchased), is attached to frame of 1/2 in. stock with screws driven into molding.

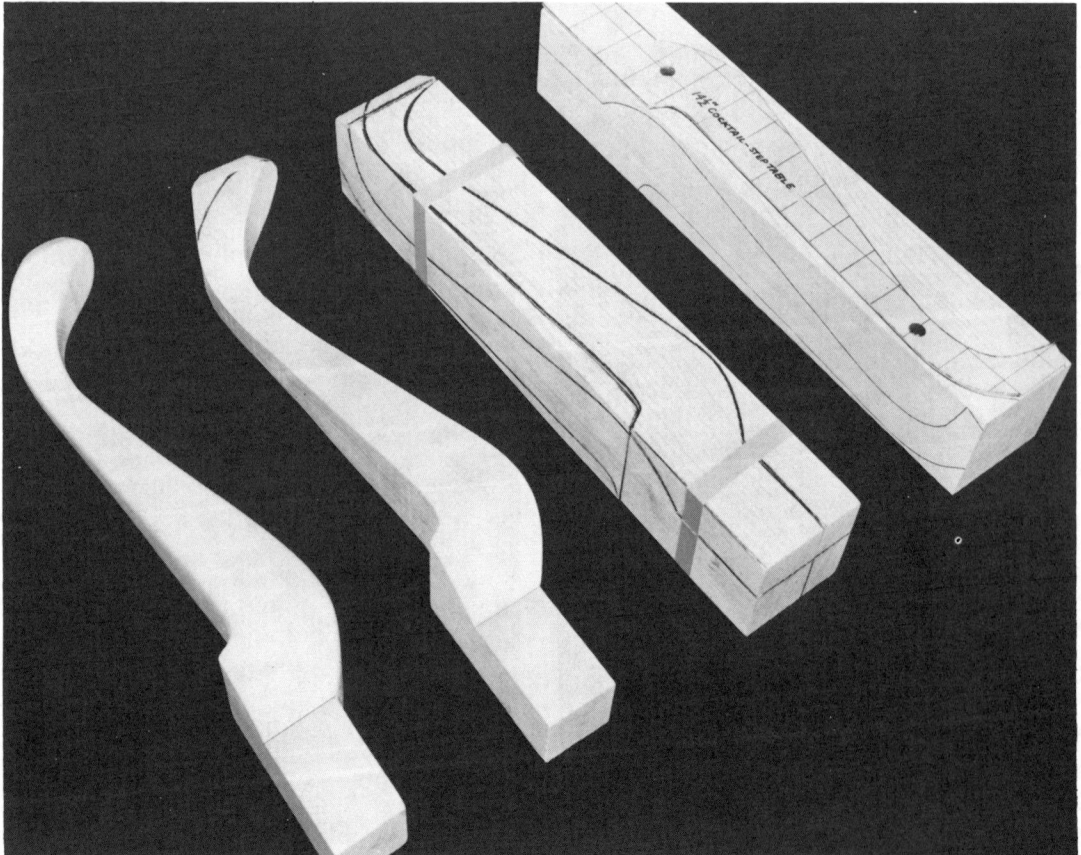
Various steps in making cabriole leg are: tracing template on block, cutting first, then second profile with stock taped back on to provide flat surface. Finally, rasp and sandpaper are used.

rounded foot, as shown in the drawing. Variations of the outwardly-curving Dutch foot were often used on Queen Anne period pieces as well. Interesting variations can be made by thinning or widening the foot, and rounding or pointing the toe. The foot with the pointed toe sometimes is called the "slipper foot" because of its resemblance to a lady's slipper.

The basic principles of making cabriole legs are presented here, and will make it possible for you to alter the style to suit an existing piece of furniture, or create your own new classic design. When you are creating a new design, first cut it from inexpensive softwood, rather than costly hardwood. A simple change of curve will alter the overall proportions drastically in some cases. Remember that changing a side profile will modify the corner profile greatly, as the corner will have much more fullness than is apparent in a side view drawing as indicated in the photos.

As to the length of the legs; this is determined by the item they will support. The usual height of legs for lamp tables is 12 in.; coffee tables and step tables generally require 14-1/2 in. legs. A fairly standard length for couches and footstools is 9-1/2 in. Tables require 27 to 29 in. legs, depending on the width of the apron or the manner in which the legs are attached. As indicated in the drawing, cabriole legs can be fitted into the corner of the apron by notching the upper part of the leg and fitting the mitered apron around it, or by using tenons on the apron to fit mortises in the upper portion of the leg. Cabriole legs also can be made without the upper, square por-

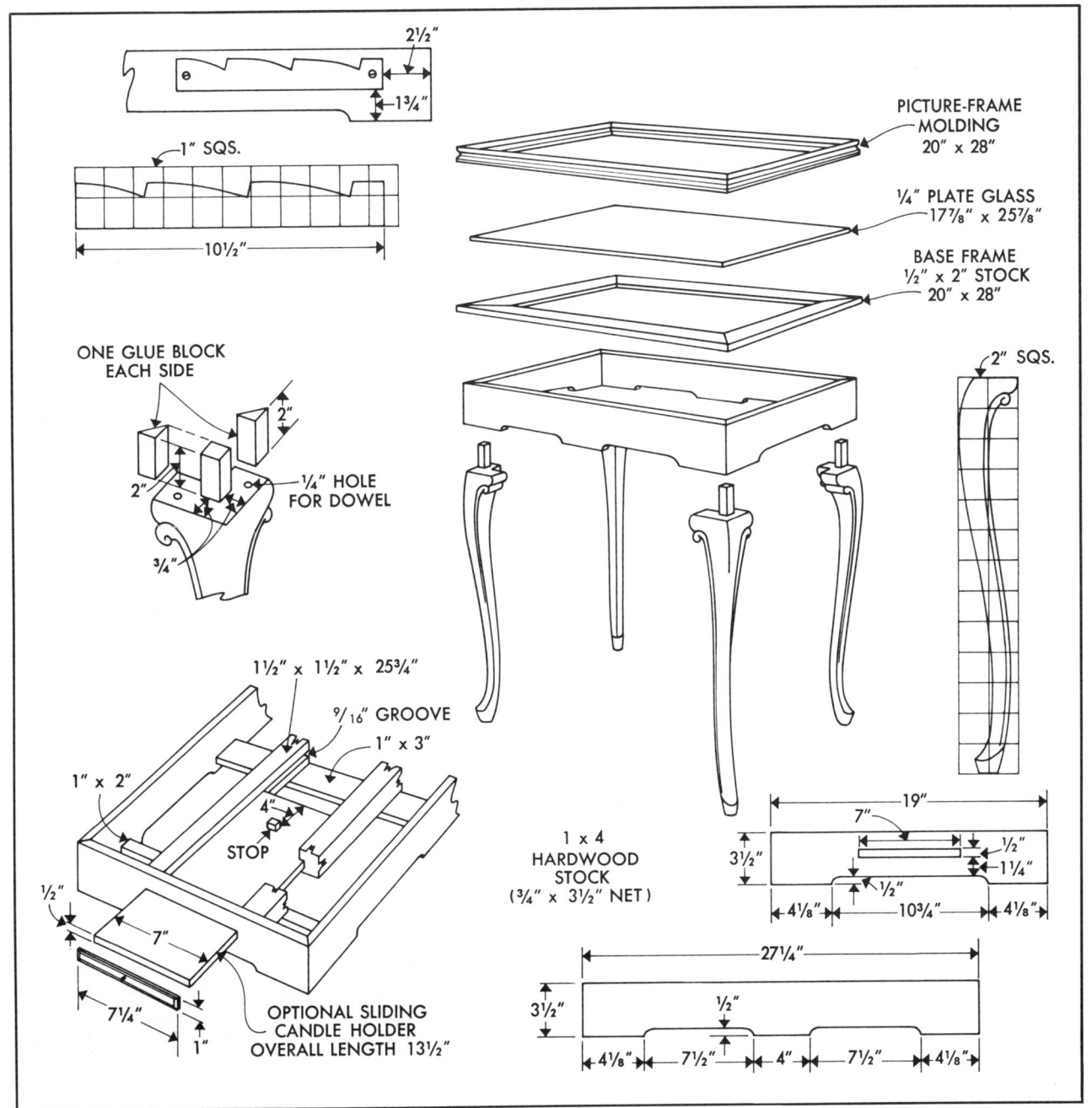

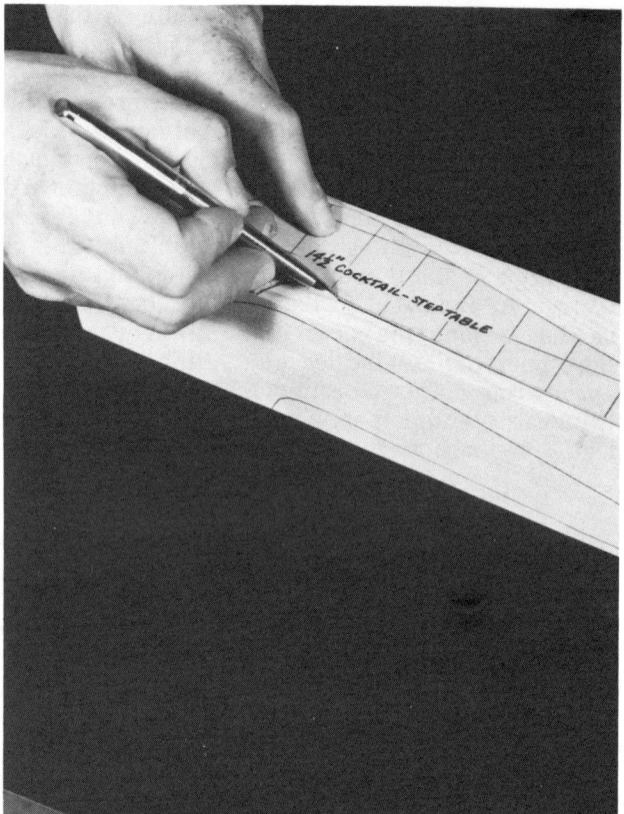
Sawing pattern for leg is traced onto adjacent sides of block that must be square so saw blade cuts at right angle to surfaces.

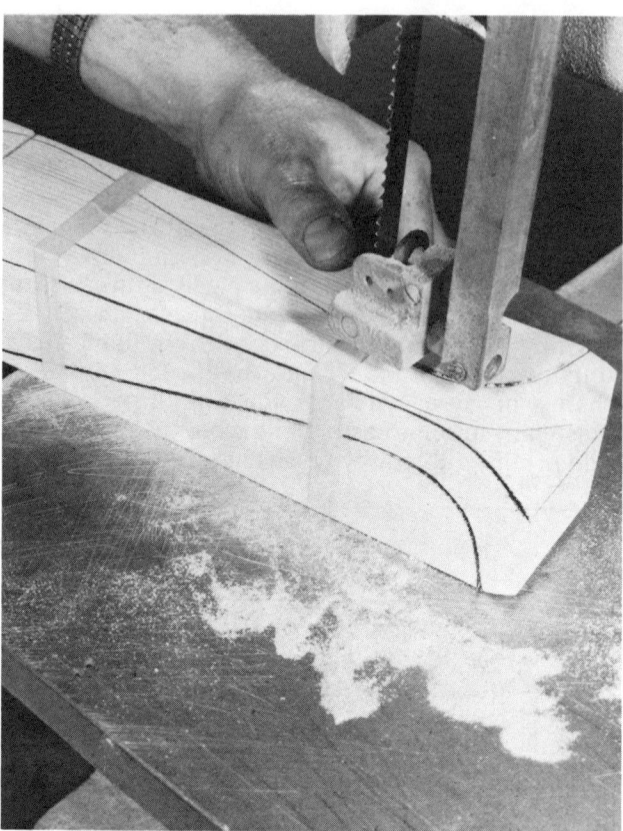
You first saw one profile, then tape waste stock back on block both to provide a flat surface on table of saw and restore lines.

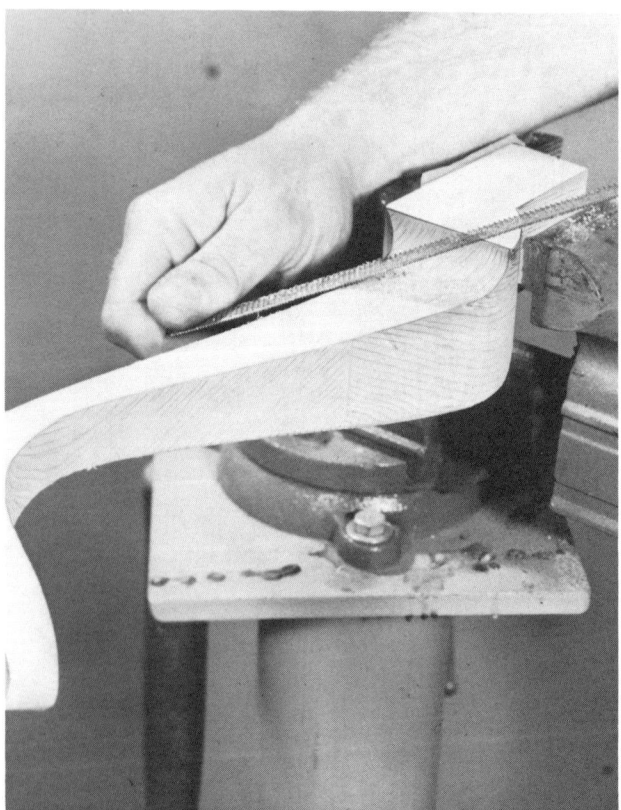
Corners of the cut-out leg are rasped to create shape shown in drawings. Final smoothing is done with sandpaper.

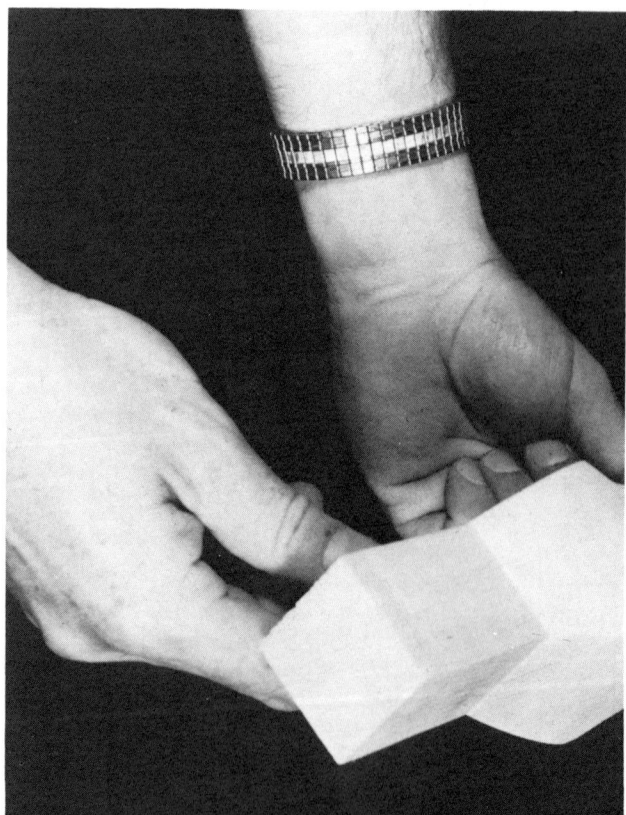
Sawing a double contour in a block produces a shape with more fullness than is apparent in a side view drawing.

tion, then doweled to the underside of the tabletop or the apron. These various methods of attachment could require a leg even shorter than the 27 in. In any case, a table should be 30 in. high when it is used for eating, as a desk or work surface.

For any of the designs shown, make a full-sized template by enlarging the squared drawing. You can make the template of cardboard, and use it to trace the shape on the wood, or you can make the pattern on paper that can be taped or cemented directly to the stock. If you want to change the design of any of the legs, it can be done by modifying the pattern. One method of determining if a design is pleasing is to make legs the exact size of the drawings shown. These miniature legs will show immediately if the design modifications are desirable for your particular project.

Shorter cabriole legs require stock 2-1/2 in. square, the longer legs will require blocks 3 in. square. Your first efforts should be with softwood; it could be expensive to practice on hardwood. If you have hardwood in thinner sizes, the required blocks can be glued-up by laminating a number of the boards to create the necessary size turning square. Use a top quality glue and be sure the boards are surfaced smoothly and are clamped tightly together until the glue sets. Be sure the blocks are square so the finished surfaces of the cabriole legs are at right angles.

Saw the leg contour on one face of the stock, then tape the scrap back on the block. This replaces the pattern lines and provides a flat surface to slide on the saw table. Turn the block 90 degrees and cut the second profile. The scrap stock now is removed and the leg, in the rough, will emerge. You now can mark the foot for shape, if it will require sawing, and saw out to shape. If the foot is simply to be rounded, a rasp and sandpaper will do the job.

The leg itself now is shaped by using a rasp to carefully round the edges. Work each leg the same amount so they will match. Finish the shaping with sandpaper, using progressively finer grits to produce a smooth surface that will look well when finish is applied.

To further assure that all the legs of a set will look the same, make templates for the cross sections shown in the drawing. Mark stations on each leg so the templates can be located in the same places on each leg.

Advanced craftsmen might want to further embellish the legs with carvings. Ball-and-claw feet on cabriole legs will require considerable skill with carving tools, and we do not recommend this task to a beginning woodworker. Anyone who can use a band saw, rasp and sandpaper, however, should be able to produce cabriole legs that can be used on any piece of period-style furniture.

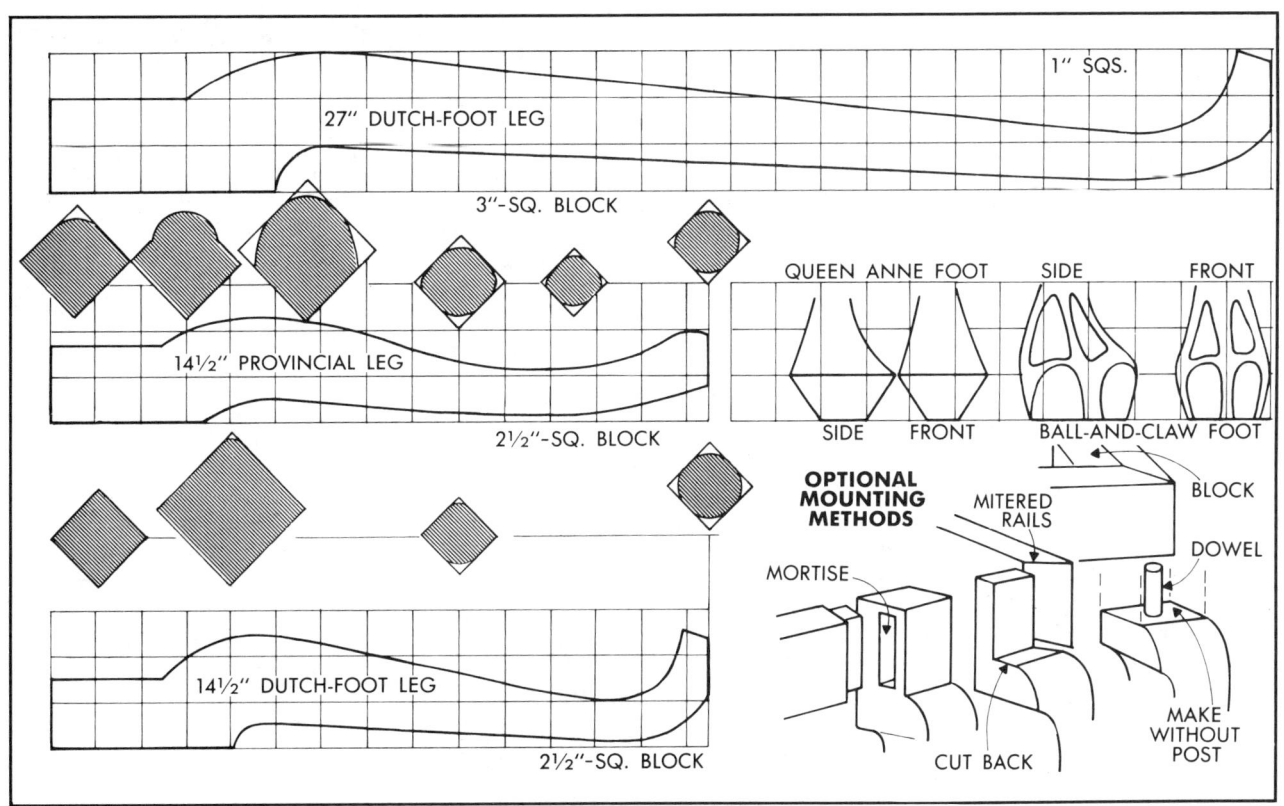

"A THING OF BEAUTY IS A JOY FOREVER."
— John Keats